Rebecca Hofmann, Christoph Dittrich

The Social Construction of Food Risks of Lower Middle Class in the
Emerging Mega City of Hyderabad/India

Emerging megacities
Dicussion Papers
Edited by Konrad Hagedorn, Christine Werthmann, Dimitrios Zikos, Ramesh Chennamaneni

Humboldt-Universität zu Berlin
Department of Agricultural Economics
Division of Resource Economics
Philippstr. 13, House 12
10115 Berlin

Tel.: +49 (0)30 2093 6305
Fax: +49 (0)30 2093 6497
www.agrar.hu-berlin.de/struktur/institute/wisola/fg/ress
www.sustainable-hyderabad.de

Contact: emerging.megacities@hu-berlin.de

The emerging megacities discussion papers are available at:
www.eh-verlag.de

ISSN print edition 2193-6927

Emerging megacities Discussion Papers are prepared by researchers working on topics in the realm of sustainable development in Megacities of Tomorrow, a research priority by the German Ministry of Education and Research (BMBF). The papers have been peer-reviewed by a board of external reviewers.
Views and opinions expressed do not necessarily represent those of the Division of Resource Economics.
Comments are highly welcome and should be sent directly to the authors.
We welcome contributions on any topics related to Megacities of Tomorrow. Further information on the submission procedure is given at:
www.sustainable-hyderabad.de/emerging-megacities

Hofmann, Rebecca; Dittrich, Christoph

The Social Construction of Food Risks of Lower Middle Class in the Emerging Mega City of Hyderabad/India

Emerging megacities Discussion Papers, Volume 5/2010

ISBN/EAN: 978-3-86741-822-5

First published in 2012 by Europaeischer Hochschulverlag GmbH & Co KG, Bremen, Germany.

© Europaeischer Hochschulverlag GmbH & Co KG, Fahrenheitstr. 1, D-28359 Bremen (www.eh-verlag.de). All rights reserved.

Cover: Photo "Metropolis", ferendus (flickr). Creative Commons License

No part of this publication may be reproduced or transmitted, in any form or by any means, electronic, mechanical, photocopying, recording or otherwise, or stored in any retrieval system of nay nature, without the written permission of the copyright holder and the publisher, application for which shall be made to the publisher.

EHV

The Social Construction of Food Risks of Lower Middle Class in the Emerging Mega City of Hyderabad/ India

Rebecca Hofmann [*], *Christoph Dittrich* [*†]

July 2010

Abstract

This paper shows how risks and threats are perceived and valuated by the socio-economic group of Hyderabad's lower class women. For this purpose, a basic introduction is given on current scientific approaches in risk theory, followed by a description of the women's socio-economic environment, as well as an overview of food and nourishment related discourses in the print media. Ensuing on this, the women speak about risks and threats from their perspective. Throughout the report, it becomes clear that perceptions and valuations are embedded in cultural and social contexts, which is why this report serves to understand risks from the emic view of the respondents.

Key words: *food risk, urban middle class, Hyderabad, India*

---

[*] Institute of Geography, Dept. of Human Geography, University of Goettingen, Goldschmidtstrasse 5, 37077 Goettingen

[†] Corresponding author. Tel.: +49 551 398 021. Email: christoph.dittrich@geo.uni-goettingen.de

1 Introduction

In 1986, the sociologist Ulrich Beck called the modern society a 'risk society' (Risikogesellschaft). It soon became a famous slogan and released a new era of scientific risk research. Hazards, for the environment or health, always have existed, but never before have they been so intensively debated by the scientific as well as the public world. Natural disasters–often severed by human maladjustment–are hereby no longer the biggest challenges, the modern society rather faces a whole array of new risky technology, applying to various fields of human life, such as nutrition and health or mobility and communication. In the last two decades, food related risks have caused several uproars in the media and public of our western society and hereby created a new awareness of these issues. BSE and bird flu resulted in the elimination of millions of livestock and in a total boycott of beef and chicken. Radioactive contaminated food ensuing from the incident at the nuclear reactor in Chernobyl or the uncertainty about genetically modified crops and dairy products shake the consumers' perceived safety as they are not directly perceptible, but represent rather latent risks of such an everyday necessity as alimentation.

Yet, to be concerned about food safety presumes an adequate and secured level of nourishment. Needless to say that people with no access to sufficient food have a different definition of food related risks. In the emerging Indian megacity of Hyderabad with its fast changing society, the people's definition of food related risk depends heavily on their economic and social position. In the words of Isabelle Milbert (2009: 234): "Risk and vulnerability structure and organize the fragmentation of Indian cities." The urban setting bears a huge diversity of risk factors, and when people rely on external input and food purchases, the nourishment of households faces manifold threats where access to good quality food cannot always be taken for granted. This exposure to risks is especially pronounced when food is not only seen as a basic condition of life, but moreover as an integral part of personal and group identity. This report, therefore, is based on newer discourses on hunger and food security which integrate a holistic perspective and hence address the issue rather as a question of *food sovereignty* where quantity and quality, but also cultural acceptance as well as religious and social expectations, are taken into consideration (see IPC Food Sovereignty 2010). Moreover, *objective* risks are perceived by individual social beings and it therefore has to be assumed that consumer uncertainties are multi-causal and based on complex decision-making processes. What is more, Ortwin Renn, a leading risk research scientist and his colleagues point out that threats do not have any effects until they are communicated in the social world (Renn et al. 2007: 20).

Objective of the study

One of the keywords of current development research and foreign aid is 'building resilience' (see Bohle 2008: 435). As such, a long term goal of the megacity project is to identify ways how to enhance the resilience of a society in terms of food and nutrition. Resilience means the ability to buffer risk, to recover from stress and a general handling of change and uncertainties (see Blaikie & Brookfield 1987; Adger 2000; Bohle 2008). It is thus seen as a strategy to mitigate future risks (Manyena 2006: 439).

> *To live with risk means foremost to learn how to active handle social change and socio-economic transformations in order to be prepared for the insecurities, disturbances and surprises in the risk worlds of tomorrow* (Bohle 2008: 435; own translation).[1]

Hence, to strengthen a society's resilience can only be achieved with a prior understanding of local risk perception, based on an in-depth understanding of the perceivers' attitudes and responses to hazards and threats which people face in their everyday life, because these attitudes, the knowledge and the overall perception also determine the terms of conduct in risk situations. However, in the intent of a holistic and emic access to the research topic, it soon became obvious that Ortwin Renn's notice on social risk communication bears more truth than anticipated, simply by the interviewees' reaction to the question of risks in their daily life, which they answered with blank faces. Thus, a different approach which distances itself from our western categories had to be applied. Therefore, this study should be seen as an amplification of existing theorem, aiming to fill the gap between present theoretical approaches and the complex reality in such a heterogeneous environment as the life of Indian urban lower middle classes. At the same time, this is a fundamental condition towards a praxis-oriented access to resilience.

After the discussion of the basic idea of vulnerability and of some relevant risk theories (Chapter 2), Chapter 3 describes the social environment of the studied group on which the interview analysis is grounded. An important aspect of an emic risk approach is the study of societal discourses on food and health related issues (Chapter 4). With the setting of local conditions given, lower middle class women speak about their risk

---

[1] *Leben mit Risiko heißt also in allererster Linie, aktiv mit gesellschaftlichem Wandel und sozio-ökologischen Transformationen umgehen zu lernen, um auf die Unsicherheiten, Störungen und Überraschungen in den Risikowelten von morgen eingestellt zu sein.*

perception, evaluation and mitigation behaviour in Chapter 5, resumed and concluded in Chapter 6.

Figure 1: Risk and benefits
Source: Bayerische Rück 1993: 42

Methodology

As indicated above, in order to understand people's reaction to stress factors and risks, their cognitive structures, rooted in the local social and cultural framework, must be recognised and analysed, which can only be accomplished through the empirical study of the living environment. For the valuation of risk perception, it furthermore has to be taken into account that this report deals with subtle risks which are – unlike natural disasters, technological faults or animal pests – not easily quantifiable through death toll or economic damage. *Objective* risks are received *individually* and *subjectively*. Herein, as well as in the latent nature of food and nutrition related risks, present study found its difficulties.

With the intent to preferably reach comparable results, two residential areas were selected according to their prevalent income range and Hinduism as the dominant religion (Chapter 3). The focus was set on the lower middle class section as their economical assets not only secure the households' basic services but also allow the purchase of costlier products at least to a certain. But for all that, they usually lack larger savings and are therefore still vulnerable to risks. The interviews were conducted with housewives in their function of risk managers in the everyday life. In psychometric studies, risk perceptions are usually assessed by statistical methods. Yet, as was outlined earlier, the perception of risks is manifold and depends on the background of the perceiver. Thus, instead of using mathematics, an open-ended qualitative study approach was chosen in order to *allow a deeper insight in the respondents' own systems of meaning* (Royal Society Study Group 1992: 106). The intensive study of the prevalent literature in the field of risk perception gave the basis for a set of interview questions. However, during the pretest phase, the questions turned out to be too far off local realities. As a consequence, interviews were kept even more open in order to discover those risk-semantics, which play a major role in the household management of the sample group without pre-given stimuli. Repetitive answers marked certain themes as more relevant than others and were thus placed in all interviews for reasons of comparison and general statements.

In October and November of 2009, 54 qualitative interviews were taken with an average duration of 50 minutes. All households, except for two families belonging to the Sikh community, were members of the Hindu religion. 34 of the women had a school education, ten of which had a college degree, 16 visited school until class ten (where standard education ends), eight respondents had left school before the eighth class. Two of the interviewees were educated young women with a college degree but not yet married. One of the two was a Muslim and belonged to the higher income class (R-52, see box three), the other was a member of the main group of lower income households (R-53). While the median age was 36 years, one respondent of this income level was a 75 years old woman (R-51) whose appraisal is summed up in box two. One conversation was held with the dietician Mrs. Radha Reddy. All women of the main group were married and had on average two children living in the household. The mean income was Rs. 14,500; three families disposed of less than that.

2 Theoretical approach

2.1 Vulnerability

What has vulnerability to do with risk research? As Chambers (1989: 2; cited in: Bohle et al. 1993: 17) depicts: "Vulnerability means not lack or want but defencelessness, insecurity, and exposure to risk, shocks and stress." Thereof, Bohle and Watts (ibid.) derive three dimensions of vulnerability:

1. the risk of exposure to crises, stress and shocks;
2. the risk of inadequate capacities to cope with crises, stress and shocks;

3. the risk of severe consequences.

It has to be noted that the capacity to manage external hazards, for example, risks and potential negative consequences, is either fortified or alleviated by given social structures, which is also called the social vulnerability of a population. Hence, vulnerability is not synonymous with poverty. While a multitude of definitions exist, in this study, the most vulnerable are considered those:

> *who are most likely and most severely exposed to possible or actual damage, injury and/or destitution*
> *whose coping abilities and strategies (...) are the least functioning, who are therefore least capable to act and react to risk,*
> *and whose opportunities and abilities to recover from the consequences of a crisis are the most limited."*
> (see Watts & Bohle 1993a, Krüger 1997 as cited in: Dittrich & Krüger 2000: 38)

In fact, risks can encounter everyone and vulnerability is a very dynamic concept, which denotes a probability of loss, in this case the loss of adequate livelihood, and the difficulties of coping with it (HDR 2007/2008: 78). Thus, to reduce the vulnerability of a population means to reduce the risks they are facing and to identify the conditions in which people encounter such risks (Varley 1994; Blaikie 1994).

The above given description indicates the interaction of geographical, social and economic conditions which Chambers (1989: 2; cited in: Bohle et al. 1993: 19; own emphasis, R.H.) further splits into "an *external side* of risk, shocks and stress to which an individual or household is subject; and an *internal side* which is defencelessness, meaning a lack of means to cope without damaging loss." In this study, the external side is only considered with the intention to identify those factors, which lead to stress on household level. The focus, however, is on internal processes and structures. To find out what makes people defenceless, those parameters, which define vulnerability have to be listed and specified. It is generally recognised that the vulnerability of an individual depends on class, age, gender, ethnicity and religion and that the capacities to cope, also called assets, vary accordingly. O'Keefe and Wisner (1983), thus, see in vulnerability the degree to which different layers of society are differentially *at risk* (as cited in: Manyena 2006: 442). Urban livelihoods, dominated by a cash economy in which the majority of food has to be purchased, are extremely vulnerable, also because the social, physical, infrastructural and political dimension can lead to a 'cumulative vulnerability' (Milbert 2009: 235). Watts and Bohle (1993) further split the dynamic of the concept into a *baseline* and a *current* vulnerability (Bohle & Glade 2008: 103). Hence, those who permanently struggle to make ends meet are trapped in an every-day or baseline vulnerability. Moreover, trends, shocks and seasonal threats can lead to a current vulnerability, which often enforces the baseline vulnerability to the point of severe crisis and catastrophes. It is hereby obvious that also those who might dispose over sufficient financial and social assets can suffer vulnerability under certain circumstances and occurrences. In case of this report, lower middle class households on the fringe of a secured livelihood still face an uncertain future when parameters change. This means their *coping capacity* (internal side), often equated with *adaptation* or *resilience*, still has to be considered as precarious.

In Lonergan's (1999) concept of *human insecurity* the link of vulnerability and risk perception is given. Leaving his reference to environmental vulnerability apart, his concept offers a connecting point in his definition of human insecurity as the result of:

1. the actual risk of exposure to stress,
2. the perception of risks, and
3. the potential coping capacity.

In stressing the importance of individual and collective perception, he takes the vulnerability approach further, bridging it with an important point of risk research: the social, economic and political construction of risk perception and mitigation (Lonergan 1999: 2; in: Kremer 2004: 39). In the following, theoretical approaches of risk research, including risk perception and mitigation, will shortly be outlined and summed up to which they relate to present study.

2.2 Risk research

In pre-modern times, catastrophes, disasters and accidents were interpreted as a divine punishment for sins committed by humanity. The earthquake and the following tsunami, which hit Lisbon on the first of November, 1775, resulted in a paradigm shift from the religious view of fate towards an understanding of man-made consequences through human maladjustment (Dombrowsky, 2008: 65). While the traditional geographical study of natural hazards and catastrophes as well as the first technological risk analyses expressed risks as the probability of events and the magnitude of consequences, the last three decades of risk research saw an increasing integration of environmental, economic and social aspects in sustainable risk management, as well as an emphasis on man-made hazards. The interdependence of various factors was also reflected in the development aid policy with its discussion in the Brundtland report 'Our Common Future' in 1987 (Dombrowsky, 2008: 70).

This orientation led to another major finding in the study of risks which gave the scientific debate a new direction and shaped it strongly: The social experience of risk is the result of cultural identity and social influences. The human being as a 'homo sociologicus' (coined by the sociologist Ralf Dahrendorf, 1958) acts conforming to socially and culturally learned codes and rules. This was taken further by Mary Douglas and Aaron Wildavsky who made an important contribution to the scientific discussion of risks in determining the *Cultural Theory*, which sees social and cultural relations as more formative than personal traits and which are named responsible for the individual's risk behaviour, classified into a set of four major world-views or *cultural biases* (fatalism, individualism, hierarchy and egalitarianism) (Douglas & Wildavsky 1983). This approach was widely resumed, adjusted and amended (see Pidgeon et al. 1992: 113). However, there were also scientists who criticised the categorisation, because an individual may be part of different social and cultural groups, especially in this age of individualisation and the pluralisation of life styles and value attitudes[2]. Of significant impact, therefrom, has been the psychological research on risk perception, which evolved at the end of the 1970s around the *Oregon Group* with Baruch Fischhoff, Sarah Lichtenstein and Paul Slovic (for further information see Slovic, 2000). Their *psychometric paradigm* is the foundation of numerous empirical studies and will be discussed later on. Nevertheless, to integrate the cultural frame is of importance to any risk analysis and was taken up by almost all scientific approaches.

In social sciences generally, several pairs of opposites serve as an advance to risk classification: objective–constructivist, individualistic–structural, cultural–systems theoretical, or contextual–organisational (Renn at al. 2007: 45). It therefore becomes clear that risk research is as manifold as are risk interpretations and Ortwin Renn, a leading scientist in this field aptly states:

> *(...), we still lack a comprehensive concept of the social experience of risk. For example, the social processing of uncertainty in a complex society. The risk field is divided in many different schools and perspectives resulting in a patchwork of approaches* (Renn & Zwick 2002: 2).

---

[2] Michael Zwick has pursued this criticism and compiled six value orientation patterns which turned out to be relevant and recurrent motives in an interview serial on normative dispositions (Zwick & Renn 2002: 54–56).

He further argues that only few empirical studies have been conducted and that they are too few to link scientific risk assessments with the individual, social and cultural perception and experience of risk. Latent risks so far were represented by illnesses or technologies such as cancer and genetically modified food, and only recently has the study of subtle risks been given a new priority in risk research. This is due to the gradual pollution of the environment, amongst other things also climate change, which increasingly bears on health and life quality (see Griffiths et al. 2009), driving the public to call for a risk concept which can be instrumentalised as an early indicator of possible long-term effects (Renn et al. 2007: 84). However, of the accomplished studies, only some were realised in developing countries (Kremer 2004: 17) and there is still a definite lack of studies on local perceptions of risks with the potential to deteriorate livelihoods.

Nevertheless, and without any claim to be complete, some common approaches to a risk definition will be outlined.[3]

2.2.1 Definition of risk

The term 'risk' is common in the daily language use and can have a multitude of definitions. It can mean a risky business, the everyday reality of crossing roads, a diminution of security (chemicals, Internet, terrorism), natural hazards, leisure-time risks etc. (Felgentreff & Dombrowsky, 2008: 19). With the lack of an explicit definition, it is important to differentiate *who* is talking under *what* circumstances about risk, thus to view it from the angle of the observer. The probability of being exposed to hazards with a possible suffering of negative consequences can act on the micro (household), meso (social groups, city) or macro level (region, nation) and can have various temporal delimitations with direct or indirect effects. Risks can be traditional/natural (floods and droughts, infectious diseases, food poisoning) or modern/self-inflicted hazards (urban air pollution, climate change, technology) (Renn et al. 2007: 15; www.who.int). Characteristics for our modern times are systemic risks, whose impact exceeds the point of origin and who furthermore demonstrate a high complexity, insecurity and ambiguity (for example climate change) (Renn et al. 2007: 176). Risk generally refers to potential, yet real consequences and is hence at the same time social construct as well as a representation of reality (Kremer 2004: 10; Renn et al. 2007: 61). This new socio-ecological perspective was, for example, applied by the German Advisory Council on Global Change (WBGU)

---

[3] For a good summary of risk approaches in social sciences, see Renn et al. 2007: 44–62. For a summary on risk approaches in the health sector see Kremer 2004.

with the intent to construct an ideal risk typology, based on Greek mythology ('the sword of Damocles', 'Pandora's box', 'Medusa', etc.) (Renn et al. 2007: 163).

Here, once again, the crucial difference in risk definition depends on the point of view: It can be seen both from a quantifiable or real, and a normative or constructivist perspective. For a long time, risk has been formalised as the product of probability and loss. For its determination in the context of old and new technologies, health or natural hazards, scientists and actuarial mathematics from insurance companies made use of risk equations such as *feasibility of death or monetary value per year or the amount of damages per occurrence probability* (Elverfeldt, Glade & Dikau 2008: 38).

However, as indicated above, risk is contingent on sociocultural structures which impact the determination of acceptable risks and it therefore has to be understood as a *normative* concept. For example, the discussion of risks in the western society took off in the 1970s, when the risks of nuclear fission presented a threat to people's perceived safety. A new awareness of health threats emerged and initiated a whole series of risk assessment studies.

To sum up, a risk can only resemble a threat when there is a potentially affected object, in this case the human being. In addition, risk research only makes sense on the presumption that the outcome is at least to a small degree influenceable (Renn et al. 2007: 20). A person always interacts in networks of formal and informal relationships, which entails that attitudes and beliefs are shaped in the framework of culture and society. Therefore, risk has to be understood as a social construct with interpretations and ascription processes regarding the risk itself as well as possible action alternatives. Ascription processes, in turn, depend on social affiliations and thus, risk perceptions and valuations may differ, depending on the social and economic status, as well as on the degree of education. It herein becomes clear that outer influences have to be taken into account, too. Professionals, authorities such as the health department and leading lifestyle philosophies play an important role in social and individual risk behaviour, which is subdivided into perception–reflection (conscious risk analysis)–and action (coping, mitigation, avoidance) (see Homburg 1995: 63; in Kremer 2004: 31).

2.2.2 The perception and valuation of risk[4]

As difficult it is to find a definition of risk, to conceptualise its perception is no easier. The Royal Society Study Group of London resorts to a very ample scope in declaring:

---

[4] For a profound review see Rohrmann & Renn 2000; Renn et al. 2007.

> *(...) the perception of risk is multidimensional, with a particular hazard meaning different things to different people (depending, for example, upon their underlying value systems) and different things in different contexts*
> (Pidgeon et al. 1992: 89).

This again adverts to the interrelation of perception with social attitudes as well as with individual experiences and collective value ascriptions, which undergo an individual judgement process. Wildavsky (1993: 203) refers to it as 'risk selection', where ethnic groups and nations come to differing perceptions of risks. Apart from that, the literature differentiates a whole list of individual or risk-inherent characteristics, situational or contextual factors of risk perception and categorises them in various ways. They all have the difficult methodological assessment in common. The following gives a summary of those factors and processes concerning the perception and valuation of risks, which contribute to the comprehension of present empirical study.

A basic subdivision gives Anja Leppin (1994: 37) who differentiates between

a) direct perception – an acute threat requires instant attention and action, and

b) indirect/analytical perception – an incident is temporally dislodged or not directly controllable.

Hence, the probability of being affected by a harmful incident, together with the potential severity, generates a subjectively perceived vulnerability, which results in a certain risk behaviour (ibid.). The evaluation of threats depends on various factors people with children, for instance, are more likely to avert risky business. And while there is generally little tolerance for not self-imposed risks, those which are judged as voluntarily taken (sometimes with a willingness to take risks as a person's character trait), known, controllable and with little catastrophic potential are usually perceived as small and bearable (for example gambling) (Jungermann & Slovic 1993: 96ff). Through the ascription and rating of such risk characteristics, a 'personality of hazards' is created which is also called the *psychometric paradigm*. Paul Slovic, one of the founding fathers of the psychological risk research goes even further and claims that "[h]uman beings have invented the concept 'risk' to help them understand and cope with the dangers and uncertainties of life" (Slovic 1992: 119; cited in: Zwick & Renn 2002: 34). If risk is purely constructed, the critique targets the sole existence of risk perception, arguing that something which does not really exist cannot be perceived either (see Brehmer 1996; in Kremer 2004: 18). Nevertheless, many scientists base their concepts on the constructivist risk approach or use it at least to explain differing risk evaluations. Similar to Jungermann & Slovic, Peter Sandman (1987) sees voluntariness, control, fairness, familiarity, dread, memorability, diffusion in time and space as some of the main factors to which laymen respond with either intensification or attenuation of risk, a process which he calls *outrage*. Moreover, the appraisal of perceived fairness in the distribution of risk and the damaging or beneficial consequences plays a decisive role. Here, Sandman (1987: 21) as well as Jungermann and Slovic (1993: 92) point to the absorbing observation that rankings of those risks which result in a number of deaths per year and of others which agitate the public are quite dissimilar from each other. One factor possibly plays the *stigmatisation*, an amended concept of the psychometric perspective which sees the negative valuation as a subjective ascription process initiated by the industrial modernisation with its ever increasing complexity of technology and knowledge (Zwick & Renn 2002: 38). While Beck (2007) comes to the opposite conclusion, namely that some people respond with belittlement or de-negation to threats, the Indian case with its technology adoring society certainly needs further studies on this topic.

The judgment of risks also seems to be governed by perceived responsibility of and trust in institutional performances that is they are entrusted with professional risk management. This applies to all social institutions (industry, political authorities, media, environmental and consumer agencies) who are involved in risk perception processes. The two which lay people have confidence in institutional performances, again, depends on their subjective experience (Zwick & Renn 2002: 46). In summary, people interpret hazards according to a whole set of preconditions, including objective and subjective risk characteristics which are ranked accordingly and which lead to the final risk estimation.

Thus, perceived risk is always dependent on the perceiver that is the decision maker and his temporal and local context. This leads to another important observation: Since risk perception is subjective, it is not detached from outer influences and cultural preconditions. This also means that the evaluation of risks bears a potential danger of over- or underestimation of indicators as the rating of risks is subject to various forces: Individual interpretation depends on personal, social and cultural experiences and is influenced by many sources from the outside. As such, the media as well as scientific and political institutions, involved with risk determination and communication, play a decisive role in forming individual and public opinions (Zwick & Renn 2002: 38). Thus, ecological disasters are often overestimated due to strong media coverage, while prevalent illnesses such as cancer and heart attacks tend to be neglected by the media as well as the public (Leppin 1994: 50). Jungermann & Slovic (1993: 93) describe an *availability* heuristic where a risk is evaluated as probable according to its attention in the media. If taken further, this can lead to the cognitive process of *toxicopy*, a medical concept, often used in environmental health studies and similar to the placebo effect, where the sole threat assumption can trigger discomforts. Nevertheless, the flow of complex information has decisive influence on people's risk evaluation, especially when risks are not experienced personally. On the other hand, however, it can also lead to uncertainty and misunderstandings, especially when not even experts agree on the estimation of certain risks (Wildavsky 1993: 207). This *signal value* (Slovic, Lichtenstein & Fischhoff 1984; Kasperson et al. 1988) of information bears the potential of splitting the society into experts, who base their judgments on conclusive scientific knowledge and laymen, who tend to follow rather intuitional and emotional aspects (Sjöberg 1998; in: Zwick & Renn 2002: 39). The whole process of filtering, reproducing and communicating risk evaluations was described by the Clark University group (Kasperson, Renn, Slovic, et al.) as *social amplification* (Pidgeon et al. 1992: 114). It is an attempt to combine psychological, social and cultural approaches which centre on the observation that knowledge of hazards and threats is to a good deal second hand and that the receiver makes his judgements based on signal values of risks which have gone through a set of *amplification stations* (Kasperson et al. 1988).

Following statement summarises all above discussed elements:

> *Human perceptions of and reactions to risk are shaped by past experience and by information and values received from sources such as family, society and government. It is a learning process that begins in childhood–when children learn not to play with fire–and is constantly updated in adulthood* (WHO 2002: 3).

Remains one more important aspect: Personal resources such as the evaluation of one's own capabilities or social networks as well as the choice of alternatives are crucial in the evaluation of risks, complying with the perception of one's own vulnerability, which affects the reaction of the person concerned and is thus a critical point of risk mitigation.

2.2.3 Risk mitigation

In reference to the internal side of vulnerability, risk mitigation means those strategies and principles, which reduce the susceptibility of hazards and threats, subdivided into *adjustments* (short-term precautionary actions) and *adaptation* (long-term adjustments within the cultural environment). This way, mitigation becomes a consecutive form of coping and is the logical deduction from risk behaviour, which ideally should conclude with social resilience as "the ability of groups or communities to cope with external stresses and disturbances as a result of social, political and environmental change" (Adger 2000: 347). The vulnerability approach attributes economic (property, work, capital), sociopolitical (institutions, social networks, social status), ecological (infrastructure, natural resources) and personal (health, education, individual capability) assets to a person's coping capacity. Yet, in the urban context, processes of change are diverse and rapid and it therefore has to be kept in mind that the coping capacity only describes the potential resilience, which can differ from actual coping (Kremer 2004: 36). This means that perception does not necessarily lead to action, a fact sufficiently shown in studies and representing a common dilemma. This is reinforced by the unknown side to a possible threat or danger, which every risk entails, because it is this incertitude which makes situations risky in the first place. Especially when talking about environmentally or alimentation induced problems, the unknown side increases due to temporal delay and dislocation of the consequences. Thus, a response is only fructuous when flexible. According to Lazarus (1968; cited in: Kremer 2004: 32), *cognitive appraisal* marks the evaluation of risk situations and can lead to either of two strategies:

a) direct action (escape or avoidance), or

b) benevolent reappraisal.

Yet, it is essential to also regard risk mitigation as embedded in social, economic and political structures and therefore, in the politics of risks, scientific expertise should be paired with social and cultural preferences to ensure a long-lasting risk management (Zwick & Renn 2002: 95). Another important perspective follows a new approach of vulnerability and risk studies: The emphasis on the people's capacity to ward off risks and vulnerability instead of just seeing the degree to which vulnerability limits them in their reactions (see Wisner et al. 2008: 13f). To further nourish the people's mitigation capability, participation in decision-making processes, based on knowledge and awareness as well as the willingness to assume responsibility in risk mitigation should be enhanced, because observing only one causal chain cannot meet the requirements to understand local risk perception and neither will lead to adequate solutions (Royal Society Study Group 1992: 122; Renn et al. 2007: 107ff).

2.3 Applicability of existing theories

In today's world of racing processes in technology, with, to give just one example, the possibilities which come with decoding genomes, risk evaluations are challenged in so far unknown dimensions (Jungermann & Slovic 1993: 103). Various disciplines are therefore engaged in risk research which enjoys increasing popularity, however without finding a common definition or approach. While some stress the meaning of norms and values, others put societal and institutional influence over personal ascriptions. Psychometric approaches, again, have been criticised for its arbitrariness due to the usage of value scales on assumed risk characteristics (Kremer 2004: 20). Especially with latent risks, however, such scales are hardly applicable. The complexity of risk assessment is also demonstrated by the interplay of various factors, however with selective attributes showing differing results in a number of studies. The temporal and local distance, for example, leads to either a neglecting or fortifying attitude towards given risks. As will be demonstrated later, the Indian-specific appreciation of future plays a major part in understanding Indian risk perception. In addition, as the religious and cultural background is very influential in the construction of risks, the Indian case has to be understood as a very complicated setting with its high diversity of major religions, subdivisions and world-views.

Taking the constructivist approach nevertheless as the basic explanation model for present study on risk perception, the author strongly emphasises that even subjective and constructed risks have an objective core, for example in natural disasters, structural changes, etc. Also, newer risk studies mostly refer to technological risks and the consequences of environmental pollution. Studies on risks in relation to livelihoods in a socio-geographical sense, however, are usually restricted to the theorem of vulnerability. The socio-ecological approach, which is currently developed and refined by Renn et al. 2007 (122ff), tries to integrate the ramifications and impacts of social valuations and actions on the natural environment. They argue that natural processes exist irrespective of our perception. Yet, the evaluation of such processes and their consequences is based on social and cultural preconditions (ibid. 132, 133). Leaving the ecological sphere aside, this moderate realism, placed in a constructivist framework, shall serve this report as the leading risk perception approach.

Last but not least, the author would like to point out that a difference has to be made between countries with varying level of development, because people in developed nations usually have a broader package of assets and thus also dispose over various technological and economical options to avoid or reduce risks (see Wisner 2008 et al.: 19), while people in less developed countries often have no or only insufficient alternatives.

3 The social environment of the respondents

As became clear in the theoretical overview, social risk research defines risks as inherently subjective even to the point where it solely becomes a concept made to help cope with the uncertainties of life. At the same time, risk is socially determined and the society with its norms and values is an important agent in perception processes and thus plays a major role in risk interpretation and definition (Wildavsky 1993: 197). If both traits–subjectiveness and social determination–are combined, i.e. if the individual person as the risk perceiver is understood as a social being, imbedded in a net of social, cultural and institutional relations, the assessment of a specific group's risk perception has to include the study of their living conditions as well as the broader cultural, economic and political context, inclusive the ruling risk communication as important factors of risk construction.

In this regard, this paper lacks–due to limited time and resources–a sufficiently detailed study of the structural economic and political conditions, which are only alluded as so far as they were brought up in the interviews. Moreover, the study was outlined to focus on the emic view of risk perceptions and valuations among Hyderabad's lower middle class women. While democratic factors are not proven to influence risk evaluation, the gender index does show a small difference. Even though there are no studies which clearly give proof of and explain a gender based risk perception, women nevertheless tend to a higher risk evaluation than men, or in rather simplistic words: women worry a bit more than men (Kremer 2004: 85).

3.1 Urban setting

People live in cities for varied reasons, amongst others because they are valued as a safe harbour where one can escape droughts and floods and where emergency programmes relieve the aftermath. Moreover, common belief is that in cities job positions are open at every corner and that life is much easier with the broad spectrum of purchasable goods as well as loosened social structures. However, also an urban environment carries many general risks, for example pollution of the air, water and streets, bad sanitation, etc. While risks related to food and nourishment are present both in rural and urban contexts, reasons come usually from very different angles: For example, farmers in the countryside end their lives due to crop failure (DC, 10.11.2009a), while more and more young city dwellers (especially women) see in suicide their last resort from social stigmatisation due to overweight or other socio-cultural issues. This is even more pronounced in cities like Hyderabad where the rapid growth features profound changes on socio-economic and cultural levels. Yet, „change is nothing new and one way to know how to be resilient to it, (...) is appreciation of this fact." This appreciation has to take place against the background of the local culture, because it "frames the way people perceive, understand, experience, relate to, and respond to the social and physical worlds around them." (Nuttall in: Crate & Nutall 2009: 297) In the urban context, the social culture becomes usually more and more monetarised, which is why the economic assets will be outlined in following, however, not without saying in advance that a sole wage classification is too static to aptly grasp the complex social and financial set-up of lower middle classes with all associated assets.

3.2 Lower middle classes

This report concentrates on Hyderabad's lower middle classes, which, although widely discussed, still lack a clear definition. In order to allow the comparison with other studies conducted in this project, it was agreed to use an income-based approach. However, this is not done without scepticism, amongst other reasons, because the National Council for Applied Economic Research (NCAER) subsumes the middle class under the huge annual income range from Rs. 90,000 up to over Rs. one or two million (1,400 - 30,000 €/year; currency taken from February, 19 of 2010; NCAER 2007)! Other scientists, therefore, prefer to avoid the juggling with numbers and simply note that India's middle classes are extremely heterogeneous and influenced by the trends of economic, social and cultural globalisation (Lange & Meier 2009: 31).

The lower middle classes, also called 'aspirers', with an income range of Rs. 90,000 to 200,000 per year (Rs. 7,500 - 17,000 per month) are marked by the ambition to leave insecure livelihoods behind and catch up with the affluent middle classes, characterised by rapid changes towards new lifestyles and consumption patterns with new demands (see Hofmann and Dittrich 2009). Product quality, diversity and individual taste become the new indicators of consumption behaviour once the basic procurement of food is secured (see Popkin 1999). However, such new standards can lead to a re-evaluation of the risk concept and the households' perceived vulnerability, especially as the group of 'aspirers' is far from being secured and thus still faces precarious situations when parameters change. Such an exposure to risk can be created either through alterations in the food system (prices, availability, and quality) or through varying assets of the consumer (income, health conditions, access).

The majority of the studied households fall into the aspirers' income range. In order to contrast the answers of that income group, some interviews were held with households below the limit of Rs. 90,000 income per year. While the majority of 45 interviews took place in one of the two main study areas, three were conducted in Falaknuma, in the South of the city, and another two in a Sikh community. The two main residential areas will now be further introduced.

3.3 Study areas: Tilak Nagar and Saroor Nagar

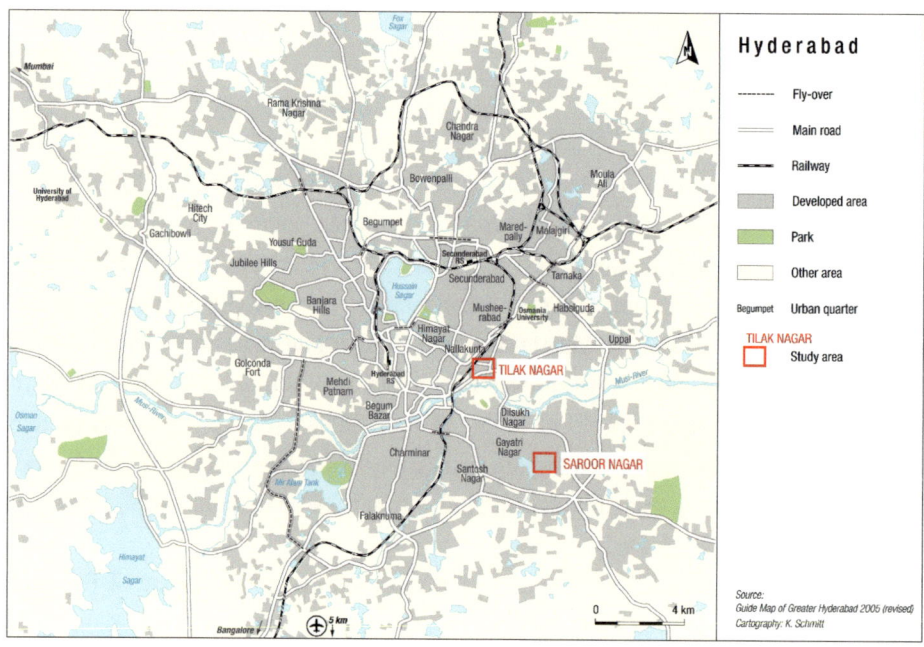

Figure 2: Map of study areas

The decision to choose Tilak Nagar and Saroor Nagar as the main study areas was based on several deliberations. First, the income of the majority of the households conforms to the above given economic definition of lower middle classes. Besides that, both areas are predominantly Telugu speaking and the general social and economic set-up of the neighbourhoods is still engrained by traditional values and customs. Yet, the main roads of the adjacent quarters Himayatnagar (next to Tilak Nagar) and Dilsukhnagar (next to Saroor Nagar), are emblematic for the fast transition from the typical gallimaufry of small shops and stalls towards big western or westernised retailers[5]. This process can currently be observed in many parts of old Hyderabad, as change is no longer restricted to the high-end areas with their predominant IT sector and the so-called white collar workers. Therefore, both study areas are well comparable.

3.3.1 Tilak Nagar

That the geographical vicinity of the 'new' Hyderabad indeed exerts some influence on the residents of Tilak Nagar, was repeatedly confirmed in informal conversations, especially with young people (20-30 yrs.) who declared to prefer Himayatnagar for (window) shopping and eating out.

Figure 3: l: Construction work on Himayatnagar Main Road. r: Fruit seller and Chinese snack bar on Tilak Nagar main road.
Source: Own source, Nov 2009, Nischalke/Hofmann Nov 2009

As suggested before, Tilak Nagar displays a different picture. Even though its main road is, compared to the winding and narrow side streets and alleys which often lead to a dead end, straight and clearly gives way to traffic, the shops lined up on either side of the road resemble a colourful picture of traditional retail dealers, further dotted with mobile street food vendors.

The study area itself entails only one small supermarket, called Mahalaxmi. Yet, only a little further down around the corner, two corporate stores, Spencers and Reliance Fresh, are situated within walking distance.

---

[5] In the case of Himayatnagar, the author herself was astonished about the magnitude and velocity of change, which took place in the seven months between the author's two field visits.

Figure 4: l: Street vendor on Tilak Nagar main road. r: Golnaka market, Tilak Nagar.
Source: Nischalke/Hofmann Nov 2009, Own source, Nov 2009

Eye-catching is the huge number of food related businesses in the studied area. Over approximately 30 hectare, 30 establishments offer food and beverages (snack bars, tiffin centres[6], curry points, restaurants, tea stalls), supplemented by sweetshops and 13 meat shops as well as over 50 kirana stores (mom-and-pop stores), whereas the smaller window-shops and mobile street food vendors were not even counted! At that come wholesale stores, milk and oil stores, fruit shops, five wine stores and last but not least the Golnaka market with even more food stalls and kiranas, stationary fish vendors and about 60 street vendors (fruits and vegetables), frequented by the residents of Tilak Nagar as well as by people from neighbouring quarters.

To demonstrate this density of local supply, which ostensibly marches on oversupply, a map section which displays the above mentioned offer in the studied area was made.

Tilak Nagar's rich food-scape is a part of a dynamic local informal economy, consisting of other small traders in the food sector such as rice and flour mills or in handicrafts such as welding, the furniture manufacturing and tailoring. Here, it has to be noted that most of the tailors are either stitching centres to which people bring their elsewhere purchased dress material, or they are subcontractors to larger clothing stores, which means that they sew collars and buttons and the like, yet do not have own designs. Others are employed by the government or have office jobs at private companies.

The housing is nearly as varied as the food stores with older independent houses along a net of narrow alleyways and newer apartment complexes. The architecture and

---

[6] Traditional Indian snacks such as samosa, bhel puri etc.

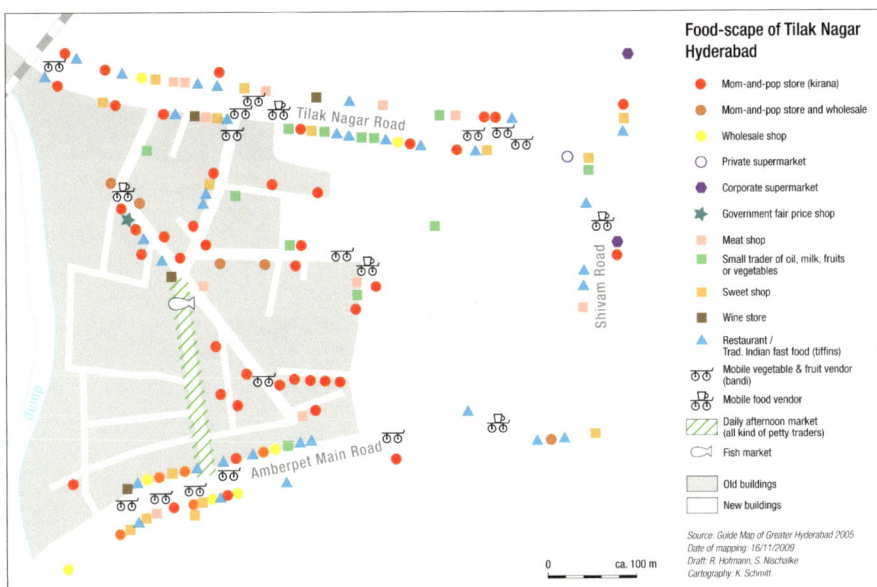

Figure 5: Tilak Nagar's food-scape

interior reaches from very small and simple to rather spacious and posh, a congruent recognisable economic pattern, however, is hard to make out.

Figure 6: Kirana store and small tailor shop, Tilak Nagar.
Source: Own source, Nov 2009

3.3.2 Saroor Nagar

The second study area does not much differ from Tilak Nagar. Situated in the East of the metropolitan area, it belongs to the Ranga Reddy district with Hyderabad as its administrative centre. It adheres to Saroor Nagar Lake, which was originally constructed in the 16th century to provide water for the irrigation of the surrounding farmland, which today is completely converted into a residential area. To its other side runs the National Highway No. 9, an important transport axis of central India. Right next to it is the Kothapet rythu bazar[7], a major shopping location of the respondents. Situated only a little further is Dilsukhnagar, a major shopping hub, which was strongly developed in the last five to ten years.

Figure 7: l: Kothapet ryhtu. r: Towards Dilsukhnagar.
Source: Own source, Nov 2009/ Feb 2008

All in all, Saroor Nagar and Tilak Nagar correlate in most parts of their general set-up. Small differences might be found in the less abundant offer of food and drink options and the absence of a daily market in the immediate vicinity. This, however, is compensated by the rythu bazar, which, albeit further away, still offers cheaper rates. Besides, Saroor Nagar is foremost a residential area and most people have to commute to their office jobs, unlike in Tilak Nagar, where handicraft and small trade in situ prevails.

Due to the homogeneity of the two study areas, from now on, both will be treated likewise without specification of the respondent's residential suburb (R=respondent). All other interviews (i.e. those conducted in Falaknuma, in the Sikh community or with others) will be identified accordingly (F=Falaknuma).

With given account of the economic conditions and the illustration of the respondents' living area, two important factors, which influence a subjective, yet socially determined risk perception, have been covered. However, on a larger and more general scale, the framework for crisis and their management are shaped by even more factors, such as the

---

[7] Producer markets with quality checks and fixed prices.

endowment with natural resources to buffer shortages, as well as policies and laws which define the stability of a system and rule the management of risks. As aforementioned, these factors were largely left aside, and instead the society itself in its role as an important agent in risk management was put in the focus, reviewed by means of following discourse and interview analysis.

4 Societal discourses on food related risks as represented in the print media

The detailed look at the risk perception of lower middle class women was framed by a discourse analysis in order to obtain a more general idea of what moves the society in relation to food and health. Thus, the print media as one voice of the society serves to identify those societal issues, which relate to risks mentioned by the interview partners. In this regard, Wildavsky (1993: 206) points to the fact that new information more likely leads to a negative estimation of threats. The availability heuristic also refers to the attention in the media with its signal value, which carries a potential of uncertainty or faulty conclusions to the reader's opinion making (see Chapter 2).

For this purpose, the two most widely circulated English daily newspapers in Hyderabad, *The Hindu* and *Deccan Chronicle* have been studied over the research period of two months (October and November 2009) with a focus on those articles pertaining to the fields of food, prices, health and lifestyle[8]. Due to lacking knowledge of Telugu, the interviewees' local language, the study had to be limited to the English press. Preliminary results, however, were cross-checked with the research assistants who confirmed that the print coverage in Telugu-media is similar, although the Western influence is slightly less noticeable.

The description of the selected discourses shall be heralded by one of the most striking observations: Albeit the proportion of western ideas and trends regarding lifestyle is quite remarkable, concerns of physical and mental well-being still seem to be largely based upon and infused with Indian spiritual traditions and its modern movements. A fine example of the topic of risks gives following excerpt from the *Emotional Fitness*

---

[8] Although the discourse analysis refers mostly to articles in the two named newspapers, other English papers also were studied, albeit to a lesser. As their contents are largely congruent with *The Hindu* and *Deccan Chronicle*, only those contributions which are especially apt to illustrate discussed issues are included in the analysis.

column 'There's no other way to live, but dangerously' (Osho foundation) in the Deccan Chronicle Magazine from the 15th of November, 2009:

> *You will have to start dropping logic a little. You will have to take a few risks. You will have to live dangerously. People who are full of fear cannot move beyond the known. The known gives a kind of comfort, security, safety because it is known. (...)*
>
> *Friedrich Nietzsche is right: he says, 'Live dangerously.' In fact there is no other way to live; one can only live dangerously. The other way is of avoiding life, not of living. It is to accept the insecurity of life, it is to accept death, it is to accept that everything can disappear at any moment. (...)*
>
> *Security is beautiful. This insecurity has a blessing in it, because if everything were secure there would be no life at all.*
>
> *The real world has to be in constant danger. That danger adds to its beauty, that danger gives a depth, that danger makes it challenging. It is only through danger that life attains to maturity, growth. One needs to be an adventurer, always ready to risk the known for the unknown.*

Here, the banalisation of danger as adding spice to an otherwise stagnating life is conspicuous, yet is not too far from the Indian way of living totally carefree into the days to come, only interrupted when people are directly confronted with problems such as will be described next.

4.1 Rising prices

The south-west monsoon of 2009 has brought only 78 % of the long period average rain and was the lowest recorded rainfall of this decade (IMD 2009). Albeit the average precipitation in South India was closer to normal, severe floods, especially in Andhra Pradesh and Karnataka left millions of people homeless and led to the devastation of major parts of the 2009 harvest. With droughts on one side and floods on the other, prices for agricultural output have soared up to an unprecedented level. Starting in October 2009, prices have continually gone up with a food inflation close to 20 % in December (TNN, 29.01.2010)! "Soaring prices take eggs off common man's menu" reads a newspaper article in November (DC, 24.11.2009). And this price increase is only an additional intensification of the general upwards trend, which is exemplified by following tables.

Table 1: Price development of Sonamasoori rice 2007-2009

Source: Sarah Nischalke, 2009

Table 2: Price development of Toor dal 2007-2009

Source: Sarah Nischalke, 2009

Sonamasoori rice and toor dal (split pigeon peas) are the preferred varieties of local staple foods and are, together with onions, the basic ingredients for every curry and therefore indispensible in the South Indian basket of goods. The increasing prices of onions and potatoes are mainly named responsible for the food inflation, but other common staple foods like dal and rice or tomatoes also have become increasingly expensive.

Table 3: Price development of onions 2007-2009

Source: Sarah Nischalke, 2009

Because the Indian cuisine is based on exactly these food items, the higher prices resemble a twofold risk:

1. Soaring prices threaten the food provision of less affluent households (hereby completely ignoring the majority of poor people), also through their impact on the Public Distribution System, which reportedly offers products of lesser quality or even struggle to provide sufficient subsidised foodstuffs which have to be restocked at the open market due to the programme's failure of allocating enough supplies, respectively due to undue distribution (Vydhianathan 2009). This is especially tragic as it also affects the vulnerable group of children who, for an adequate alimentation, depend on the midday meal scheme at government schools. Yet, school meals are either limited in quantity, diluted or certain ingredients are substituted. One example is the distribution of soy milk instead of cow milk, which is however widely rejected by the children as they are not accustomed to the taste (The Hindu, 13.11.2009a).

2. As indicated above, taste plays an important role in the Indian food culture. Hyderabadis not only tend to value taste over health, their sense of belonging is also deeply rooted in the local and regional cuisine (see Hofmann 2009). For example, the people of Hyderabad stress the importance of rice, both in terms of nutrition and identification: *If rice is there, everything is there!* (R-35) A plate full of rice is considered a wholesome meal, yet, one headline reads: "Centre

[of the Public Distribution System, R.H.] refuses rice for YSR's scheme [welfare scheme promoted by the former chief minister Dr. Y.S. Rajasekhar Reddy, R.H.] – Delhi gives wheat, AP says it won't serve purpose" (DC, 15.10.2009a). Hence, the symbolic appraisal of food should not be neglected in a study on subjective interpretations of food related risks. This is further illustrated by the example of sugar. Because sweetness is a trait of divine food, this usually much sought after commodity during the festive seasons in spring (*sankranti, holi*, etc.) and autumn (*ganesha, dasra, divali*, etc.), in 2009 has failed to meet the demand of previous years and this way accentuates the gravity of the situation.

Figure 8: Newspaper cartoon
Source: DC, 23.11.2009

The monsoon of 2009 with its concurrent droughts and floods prevail in the public opinion as the main causes for the price rise. Some merchants even seem to take advantage of it and put an extra one or two rupees on actual prices. Extreme examples are prices for goats and sheep, which have sky-rocketed ahead of this year's *Bakrid*, a Muslim festival of sacrifice where families slaughter a domestic animal[9]. While merchants hike the prices of livestock every year during Bakrid, in 2009, they excuse the exorbitant rates with the preceding floods (DC, 28.11.2009). Some Hinduists, too, see the reason for the price development on religious grounds and blame it among other things on *Karteeka Masam*, a sacred lunar month around November, during which devout people restrict their diet to vegetarian food. In a similar direction goes the argument that the

---

[9] The meat is divided in three parts of which the family eats one third, while another third is reserved for relatives or friends. The last third is given to the poor as a gift and is, together with other Islamic festivals, which include the contribution of food to the poor, therewith an important mitigation strategy for needy urban settlers.

high price of toor dal has pushed consumers towards pesalu (green gram) and other less common pulses (dal), which made these products more costly, too (The Hindu, 13.11. 2009). Nevertheless, climate change, in relation to the irregular monsoonal events, is a perceived cause for failing crops (The Hindu, 22.10.2009) and this way also an indicator of an increased awareness of it.

Altogether, according to the Prime Minister's economic advisory council, "managing food prices will be the biggest challenge in the short run." (DC, 23.10.2009a). The heading "Food crisis stares at state" (DC, 29.10.2009), however, seems to adhere to a perceived paralysis of the officials, and the public does not necessarily trust in the government's capabilities or even willingness to manage the situation.

Figure 9: Newspaper cartoon
Source: The Hindu, 07.11.2009

Moreover, the state has to struggle with many structural problems, for example labour shortage in the agricultural section. Rice, with costly inputs and a workforce mainly aged 45 plus, is even titled "a suicidal crop" (Pheroze 2009). Pheroze further reproaches the government with its call for a complete mechanisation of the agricultural production, which small farmers however cannot accomplish. For him it is clear that "[w]ithout subsidising labour, agriculture cannot survive. Shunning food crops for cash crops is a serious threat to food security" (ibid.). One suggested strategy is to encourage rice cultivation in tribal areas and to increase their subsidies for basic agricultural commodities (The Hindu, 23.11.2009a). For the *Kharif* season of 2009 (monsoon crops, autumn harvest), a 30 % reduction in production was expected due to the climatic events. Thus, the government has decided to increase production in the next season, also due to higher prices for super fine rice (DC, 15.10.2009b). It even declared a crop holiday for the coming *Rabi* season (winter crop, spring harvest) in view of drying up rivers which also affects the output in *Kharif* season (DC, 19.10.2009). At the same time, the government decided against the import of rice, arguing that it has enough stocks to manage the demand and rather blames the chain of intermediaries of pushing prices[10] (The Hindu, 17.11.2009; DC, 21.11.2009). Meanwhile, the Hyderabad and Secunderabad Retail Dealers' Association complains about the "tremendous pressure from the government to reduce prices. But no one does business for losses." (The Hindu, 13.11.2009a) In the forerun of the GHMC (Greater Hyderabad Municipal Corporation) elections on the 23rd of November 2009, this issue was also taken up and instrumentalised by election campaigns with political candidates warning the voters against certain parties if they do not want prices of essential commodities to rise beyond reach of the common man (The Hindu, 13.11.2009b).

To temporarily buffer the lower classes' burden of rising prices to at least some extent, mobile rythu bazars started to cater poorer residential colonies and slums (The Hindu, 15.10.2009). Furthermore, it was announced that green peas will be reduced in price and supplied through the Public Distribution System to offset the use of toor dal. Yet, the food inflation obtains an explosive potential not only for the lower classes, but also for the common man as demonstrates this letter to the editor:

The 2 Rs. per kg rice scheme is not feasible in times of recession. The price should be fixed at 10 Rs. per kg. Politicians should educate people so that they work hard and earn a living rather than being given freebies (Sukumar; DC, 16.10.2009).

Other suggested solutions are ultra-modern grain storage facilities, which demonstrate the Indian passion for technology. The article's author seems to be ashamed by his nation, which has "the largest number of hungry persons in the world". Structural and systemic aspects, however, are not even taken into consideration. A possible price reduction in the near future is not very likely, because after a slight decrease at the beginning of the year 2010, prices are again on the rise (TNN, 29.01.2010). This will make those families with limited income and savings (if they are not already exhausted after the price increase in 2009) even more vulnerable.

---

[10] Middlemen hinder fair prices both for the consumer and the producer. To help small farmers who are often not aware of current prices, the Tamil Nadu Agricultural University developed a new SMS service, which provides the daily prices. Currently, this system is tested on several markets around India (Prabu 2009).

4.2 Food safety

One of the most important principles in Indian kitchens is purity. Freshness and cleanliness are values deeply embedded in the religious customs and are strictly adhered to the diligent purchase, preparation and storage of food (see Hofmann 2009). They play a decisive role in people's eating culture at home as well as outside. The importance of it was clearly stated by the respondents (see Chapter 4) and also has a strong voice in the print coverage: "Unhygienic food joints: pose health problems" (DC, 02.11.2009a)[11]. Serving stale food in unhygienic conditions is a reality of many eating joints in Hyderabad and albeit condemned by the Indian consumer, the municipality lacks strict regulation as well as adequate resources. At the time of this report writing, the newly opened Urban Health Centre, run by Dr. Mala Rao, is engaged in setting up regulations for the Food Safety Standard Act of India, in which not only inspection officers but also restaurant managers and even street vendors shall be trained according to their business (interview with Dr. Mala Rao, 25.11.2009). The lack of sufficient sanitation inspections is broadly expounded in the media and echoes in the public's opinion. The government's pretention of dismissing the issue as non- relevant, especially during election campaigns is surprising given the high estimation of the purity value in the Indian culture.

Another story angle, which causes much public upheaval, is the widespread threat of food adulteration, either from imported foods with untrue labelling (mostly from the southeast Asian region; Oppili & Kannan 2009) or as a bad practice by local merchants or chefs to enhance their gaining. Special indignation triggers the regular occurrence of adulterated ghee (clarified butter), an indispensable ingredient and topping in the Indian kitchen, as well as of edible oils. Again, the municipality is held responsible as they do not provide adequate surveillance, not even in known Hyderabadi centres of oil adulteration, which are listed in one article (Mukherjee 2009). It is therefore recommended to only buy packaged oil from prominent departmental stores (DC, 01.11.2009), which, however, is usually also more costly. An even more helpful advice is to mix hydrochloric acid and sugar with ghee and if it turns red, it is adulterated and should be reported. The impracticability speaks for itself (Mukherjee 2009).

Another discussion has gained quite a dramatic tone: "Bt brinjal can awaken a sleeping poison" (Sahai 2009); "Bt threat to native brinjal" (Akbar 2009). Bt brinjal–genetically modified eggplants–are seen as a threat to taste, health, the environment and biod-

---

[11] In spite of the fear of food contamination and its pretended denial, Hyderabadis love their street food, which proofs following headline: "The Chinese delicacies that Hyderabadis swear by are the ones sold on road side Chinese kiosks. Spicy, hot and tangy, these eateries not only cater to the *desi* tastebuds, but are also easy on the pocket." (DC, 15.11.2009; also see Hofmann 2009).

Figure 10: Food safety
Source: Bayerische Rück 1993: 24

iversity. The hybrid Indian culture, caught between a deep affection of modern technology and traditional values, participates very emotionally in the debate, and the Deccan Chronicle even claims it to be a "vegetable war" (DC, 22.10.2009a). It continues with mentioned discrepancy: "The DC debate: Bt brinjal is a good idea, it will help enhance food production" (ibid). Indeed, some argue with the heavy losses Bt cotton brought to many small farmers which was a clear set-back for the otherwise technological enthusiastic Indians, yet another point seems to activate the public even more: "Four thousand years after it entered the Indian kitchen, the all-time favourite, brinjal or eggplant, may soon shed its traditional flavour." (Akbar 2009)

Here again, the significance given to food as a striking trait of Hyderabad's culture becomes obvious. With the fast development of the city, it is no surprise that its people are caught in the dynamic of extending and experimenting with traditional values and habits and new elements from the western cuisine and food culture, a trend which will be further outlined now.

4.3 Changing lifestyles and new eating habits

The increasing pluralisation of lifestyles is an aspect colourfully depicted by the media, whereat it is conspicuous that this change is no longer restricted to the upper classes, yet it becomes more and more acknowledged that it slowly also infiltrates groups in the middle class sector. Food, of course, plays–next to fashion and society–a prominent role in this dynamic scenario. Indianised recipies for typical American and European occasions such as Thanksgiving or Christmas are widely circulated through magazines and supplements and are eagerly collected by women. And when a Dr. Rajiv (2009) notes that "[i]t's not all about junk–Contrary to common belief, some food from the West are healthier than what cooks in Indian kitchen", the women's' interest is aroused. Given the fact that children are the ne plus ultra in the Indian society, some articles rather read like corporate advertisements, for example: "The arrival of pasteurised, no-sugar-added, untouched-by-hand, fortified fruit juices makes it possible to give your child the next best thing to a whole fruit." The article further promotes cornflakes and cereals to also increase the milk consumption. Chapatti, on the other hand, are described as just as good, however time-consuming in their preparation, a prominent aspect which will be further discussed in chapter four.

Advertising, however, is not the only way the media exerts influence. 'Planet Food' is a much liked TV programme, watched by housewives as well as girls waiting to get married. Nevertheless, according to the newspaper, this is not enough: "The city is yet to wake up. Be it food, fashion or film, Hyderabad is often the last metro to wake up to lifestyle trends. The city catches on to everything at a snail's pace, lament prominent Hyderabadis." (Chatterjee 2009a) This aptly reflects the dynamic, described by journalist as "a society rooted in culture and tradition and change takes time. But that does not mean we are unwilling to experiment. While speciality cuisine restaurants have been a rage in the country for a while now, they are still not big here. And the ones that are present are not up to the mark." (ibid.) Grievance over this, of course, is on the wealthy side, because only affluent people can partake in the flow of new pleasures. Nevertheless, an impression of how drastic the society is changing gives the article "Catching food trends–Chefs and journalists thrash out the debate about Indian culinary trends" (The Hindu Metro Plus, 17.11.2009), in which wine is discussed as a culinary companion to the Indian cuisine. In this context, it is important to keep in mind that in the traditional Hindu society, the consumption of alcohol is seen as strictly condemnable and only recently it has found its way on the menu of the newly rich and cosmopolitan urban elite. "The recent social and economic changes in the country are paralleled by a steady increase in the production and use of alcohol manufactured by the organised sector. (...) The pattern of consumption in India has changed from occasional and ritualistic use to social drinking and has become an acceptable leisure activity. (...) While drinking is portrayed as a consequence of poverty, it is also associated with relative affluence." (Jacob 2009). The augmentation of articles on wine displays this new valuation as a sophisticated and urbane indulgence and it nearly sounds disappointed that it still "has a long way to go", because for "Indians, eating and drinking are two separate things" (The Hindu Metro Plus, 17.11.2009). And while the urban elite turns more and more into wine connoisseurs, illicit alcohol, produced by adding chemicals, is the cheap alternative which attracts poorer people, causing great health hazards and social problems such as domestic violence, suicide, traffic accidents, etc. Yet, taxes on alcohol are a major source of revenues for the government and it is therefore hardly surprising that new permits are issued to enhance production in private distilleries as the "demand for liquor outreached the supply level" (The Hindu, 25.11.2009a). Nor does it astonish that nearly 200 of the 1,300 candidates contesting the GHMC elections are either connected to wine shop merchants or are shop owners themselves and that they have stocked alcohol for later distribution among potential voters (The Hindu, 23.11.2009b). The prohibition of any alcohol sale during election days appears at the most as a weak intent, and as long as industry sponsored advertising is that much stronger than the poorly funded health campaigns (Jacob 2009), not much will change. In general, the consumption of alcohol in the upper classes has become fashionable, yet more traditional families would still not openly talk about it, although this does not mean that all middle class men (and some women) abstain from it.

4.4 Concepts of beauty and health

Side effects of new eating and drinking habits, the increasing rate of obesity and its contrarious trend towards slim figures are widely discussed in the media. The 'software syndrome' and the 'eatertainment', driven by the corporate sector are named responsible for ever larger numbers of obese city inhabitants, especially those below the age of 30 (Rajendra 2009; The Hindu, 21.11.2009). Although, until recently, the problem was foremost restricted to the more affluent stratum, this is changing with higher levels of disposable income, paralleled by the availability of cheap products offered by western corporations: "The corporate sector was cashing in on the availability of higher food and increased income levels of even lower middle class families by effecting behavioural changes in the matter of food intake." (The Hindu, 21.11.2009) To countervail the alarming trend, free obesity camps are announced regularly and fitness became the new quality criterion of a modern lifestyle with fitness clubs mushrooming all over the city, promising the perfect body. Yet, most of the here interviewed do not dispose over the extra money to pay the membership fee, thus their exercise is restricted to daily walking and yoga. Some middle class youngsters, however, take on to starving days in order to look slim and get intoxicated on alcohol quicker when money is limited. With this, they also ensure to keep down the double calorie intake through food and alcohol (DC Magazine, 27.11.2009). For the young professionals with little time but enough disposable income, diuretic pills are easily available over the counter (DC, 10.11.2009b). Albeit side effects are listed and doctors' warnings cited, most articles are far from treating the issue with the appropriate seriousness and simply advise the readership to avoid such pills in certain circumstances, for example in combination with migraine medication or other pain killers. Unfortunately, the new consciousness about weight and general appearance also leads to an ever increasing occurrence of depression among adolescents. It is frightening that this is further fuelled by the–if at all only marginally criticised–news coverage on trends such as the figuratively described 'thinspiration', an online subculture which motivates people to loose weight, no matter what it takes (Chatterjee 2009b). So far a trend dominating among western celebrities, it gives an alarming example of how influenceable the media can be, and a more sensitive handling, including a well-founded awareness creation certainly is indispensible to counteract such trends. The complete re-evaluation of beauty is not only exemplified by the renouncement of the formerly valued corpulence as a sign of wealth, but also becomes evident in the depreciation of age. Age, no longer seems to be as respectable, but the media tries to turn it into an 'ageorexia' (Reddy, G. 2009). While this discourse as well as others on modern or western lifestyles used to prevail mostly among better up groups of society, they have nowadays also reached lower classes and are eagerly taken up by housewives and girl teenagers, which strive for the glossy world. They take the truth in media for granted and are quickly caught by lines such as "Want to stay trim? Just eat lots of tomatoes, says a new study" (The Hindu Magazine, 22.11.2009).

The income class studied for this report is just about to make the transition from belonging to the precarious lower classes to a more secured middle class section with an increased and diversified diet as a typical indicator. And while obesity has only started to find its way into the lower middle classes' awareness, diabetes has been on the agenda for quite a while. Hyderabad is considered the capital of diabetes with an affected adult population of 16.6 % (The Hindu, 14.11.2009). The press coverage is dense and reflects the seriousness of the situation, also linking it to newer problems such as obesity (DC, 25.11.2009).

Other health problems mentioned by the interviewees are vector-borne diseases such as malaria and dengue fever. Hyderabad has seen a tremendous spread of viral fevers in 2009, which at least partly is claimed on the economic recession with about 1,000 semi-built or deserted houses in the city. Broken bottles, empty tins and barrels with stagnant water strewn over construction sites offer perfect breeding grounds for mosquitoes (DC, 22.10.2009b). While the local climate with its high temperatures and the monsoonal precipitation already results in a high susceptibility to these communicable diseases, it becomes even more prominent with rising temperatures due to global climate change (DC, 23.10.2009b; Mukherjee 2009). In this relation, Sudhakar Reddy (2009b) draws a rather negative picture: "AP [Andhra Pradesh, R.H.], victim of climate change." He further warns that "Hyderabad is not prepared for even 10 mm rainfall and the disaster preparedness and mitigation is sub-standard."

4.5 Concluding reflection

Quite noticeable is the large number of references to 'experts' and articles written by people who hold a doctoral degree. These articles are, more often than not, difficult to understand, without specific expert knowledge or insufficiently outlined. For example, one article in the Deccan Chronicle (02.11.2009b) talks about how excessive drinking of soda damages the kidneys. Curiously, only women seem to be prone to this health hazard. Also, healthy and nutritious alimentation as well as hygienic practices are seen as good defence mechanisms against the infection with vector-borne diseases such as malaria or dengue fever (DC, 16.11.2009). Often, foreign studies are transcribed into an Indian context, totally ignoring the differing cultural, economic and climatic realities. Consequently, advices such as to assure the intake of vitamin E, has to be put into perspective when looking at the displayed foods which, although rich in this vitamin (whole-grain bread, cheese, asparagus), are all but enclosed in the traditional South Indian food menu (Hyderabad Times, 17.11.2009).

With given examples in mind, it becomes understandable how this leads to the fallacies and half-knowledge answers of the respondents. It is furthermore alarming that the majority of press articles does not at all or only insufficiently inform and educate people on practices of reducing weight or health supplements! Yet, western lifestyles are no longer freed from any critique and the fact that the media plays a decisive role in forming the public's opinion on nearly all aspects in life also carries an enormous potential to educate and create awareness among the audience. For example, through their popularisation, certain values and trends can be made socially acceptable or even desirable. On a large scale, environment or social movements could be successfully promoted. On a small scale, little trends like "[v]alue fashion retailing becomes fashionable" (Chengappa 2009), could help to overcome the shame of appearing in cloths from the last season and hence help families to save the money for more necessary things. Additionally, in case of serious crises, like the price increase or food shortages, the media can issue early warnings and thus trigger the people's mitigation behaviour (Swaminathan 2009).

5 Risks – exposure and handling as reported by lower middle class women

As discussed in Chapter 1, studies on risk perception until this day are mostly done on technology in the developed world or on natural hazards in regions prone to them. India is both a technology adoring country and stage of terrible natural disasters. This study, however, is concerned with food and nutrition related risks in the Indian cultural environment of lower middle class women in a highly dynamic urban setting. Thus, in this 'geography of risk', the question of interest is how households reproduce the social experience in terms of food, nutrition and health. Housewives are seen as the managers of risks in the everyday life, however, as the women have to deal with such occurrences on a daily basis, she recognises latent risks not necessarily as such: "We ignore routine problems usually, but now that you ask, children these days have white hair and knee pains in their thirties and the hair falls out. It's due to the chemicals in food" (R-46). In the terminology of risk research, the average housewife is a lay person and an expert as well. The sources she withdraws information from are likely to have strong influence on her perceptions and valuations. Coping and mitigation behaviour have to be interpreted within her personal capabilities and range of action. Moreover, it was repeatedly shown by now, that the scientific literature cannot be contextualised or simply transferred to just any cultural frame. Hence, in order to understand the risk assessment of lower middle class women in urban India, emic views and values have to build the basis of such an analysis. This is further backed up by the first findings of the pre-test in which it soon became obvious that the general reaction towards risk is far from being a critical calculation of benefits and drawbacks. Instead, the first and overall statement was that they are not facing any risks or threats at all! Having their precarious socio-economic situation in mind, such a positive response sounds surprising. With rising prices for basic food commodities, problems of frequent food adulteration and so forth, it seems very unlikely that these women really are freed from any risks in their daily life. They moreover show adaptive behaviour, thus, it seems rather to be a question of what they identify as risks and what do they simply consider as daily routine. Under such circumstances, it seems advisable to integrate local beliefs and convictions and to examine to which extent people tolerate given threats, respectively when they turn from simple coping behaviour to mitigative action. Box 1 (consisting of fragments and general statements from the interviews) gives a first impression of the women's routine concerning food, before following analysis will treat the topic in more detail.

Box 1: Impressions of a family's diet

Once a year, we buy rice, chillies and turmeric from our relatives in the village. They grow it naturally there, without any chemicals. Once a month, my husband takes the two-wheeler to the wholesale market to buy pulses. We always go to the same merchant, because he gives us good quality at a reasonable price. Before we had the fridge, I went every other day to the nearby market to get vegetables, now I go once a week. I check for the quality and the price. With the increasing costs, I prefer cheaper products such as leafy vegetables. I generally don't buy from bandis or kiranas, because they don't care about hygiene. Sometimes we buy fruits for our children. They need the energy, but more I can't afford.

We hardly eat outside, because it's costly and you never can be sure about the quality and hygiene. At home, I process everything myself and, although there is a small loss in taste, I use the electric mixer, because it doesn't take as much time. Ready-made mixes are of low quality and have no taste. Once a week, I make Maggi for the children, because they like it and the advertisement says it is healthy. The children like noodles, burgers, etc. So they ask my husband's brother, who they are very close with. He will buy it for them and bring it home. But they have to hide it from their father, because he says it's all food poisoning and we'll have to spend money on the doctor. And if I complain about it to my husband, it's bad for the relationship with the uncle. Yet, I also feel bad about the money and the health. But good relations in the family are more important. Nevertheless, money is tight these days, especially at the end of the month. To adjust, we try to cook the exact amount and change our recipies. So now, instead of curries and dal, we use the spicy ingredients with dal atta [flour]. We also cook a liquid with mirchi [chilli powder] to be used with rice and chapatti. We use all the spices for a good and different taste. In this way, I prefer the village where I lived until my marriage. The environment was better, we had fresh vegetables, which we would cut and cook whenever we felt like it. They were also better for the health, because they didn't have any chemicals in them. In the city, we have less energy, because we have less fresh vegetables. We never have fresh vegetables here, because they are all stored. They use chemicals, because they have to grow fast and of larger quantity. On the other hand, in the city, we don't have a water problem and many hospitals.

5.1 Awareness and perception of Indian middle class women

An important aspect to begin with is to understand that the Indian middle class woman defines herself not as an independent or even self-centred individual, but always in relation to her family. Her social role as a wife, mother and daughter in-law and therefrom also her frame of worries is clearly defined: *I think, my husband should get more money and my children should be good. They should have a bright future with good jobs. If they are individually perfect, everything will result well. I should maintain the house* (R-39).

Although college education for women is standard today and modern or western values incessantly creep into the society, lower middle class women are still caught in socialisation processes in which a married woman's scope of duties is clearly on household and family scores. The husbands' opinion on the women's role as well as the relation to their wives determines a woman's acting range. One respondent from a relatively liberal household explained: *Others are totally dependent on their husbands; they don't have any money, knowledge or exposure* (R-31). Some women are disconnected from the outer world to such an extent that their only source of information is the husband, the parents in-law and to a certain degree also the neighbours. The woman's knowledge totally depends on what others wish to share or not. This became obvious in the fact that some women, whose husbands do the shopping, had no idea about the price increase, which, of course, also has implications for risk behaviour: *It very much depends on the husbands, if they don't allow the women to do anything, then she's helpless* (R-39).

Hence, albeit young women might be inclined towards a modern lifestyle and the wish of working in their field of study, they forego such ambitions in favour of their traditional role as it is expected from their families. Instead, they project their wishes on their future family in-law and hope for a liberal husband as much as a 'modern' mother in-law. One girl explained: *I for myself worry about a job. Will I marry into a family which lets me work?* (R-01) Other girls who are already married also commented on their desire for a job once the children are old enough: *I have worked before as a teacher, but stopped for the children. Later, I would like to work again to earn some money, but now the preference is on the children* (R-15). The double burden of taking care of the household and pursuing a job usually means that the woman has to get up in the early morning hours to do her domestic work before she goes to the office. This is definitely manageable and quite common among upper class women which, however, have the help of housemaids and the necessary economic assets to frequent restaurants, curry points or they resort to ready-made meals (see Hofmann 2009). In the still very traditional lower classes, a woman usually does not have the freedom to pursue her own ideas, the ranking order is quite clear: *The kids come first. Every married Indian woman thinks only about her children. I have a real passion for work and I'm still studying, but children are more important. They are my responsibility. Mentally, a housewife thinks only of her children's' health. A working lady has to divide the time between the job and the family. I want to work because I want to get my children admitted to a good school and with me working we could save money for it. I have office experience, but the family and my husband want me to work as a teacher as the timings and holidays are more suitable to manage both the job and the children. Unfortunately, I'm least interested in teaching* (R-31).

However, although some families need the extra money, traditional values are deeply rooted and even women with a college degree showed little respect for those who do not adhere to their traditional social role: *Working ladies are interested in junk food and thus get obese* (R-31). This outstanding position of children in Indian families will now be further outlined.

5.2 The importance of children and their schooling

We give our preference to our children and their needs (R-12). As indicated above, this preference determines risk perception and coping behaviour to a high degree. The most worrisome points were listed by one mother: *Most important for my children's' life is: education - job - marriage. Not before my son will get a good job and my second daughter is educated and gets a good family, will I stop worrying* (R-40). Thus, the future and fate of the offspring is loaded with a dread factor which enforces the evaluation of threats in a negative manner and the whole energy and attention is concentrated on the children, especially when it comes to food[12]: *The most important to me, concerning food, is that it is according to the children's' wishes* (R-04). This also leads to tensions, because the children are subject to outer influences such as advertising, often targeted at the consumers of tomorrow and they are confronted with social pressure and ever increasing requirements: *The children demand for variety, but everyone wants the same quantity, so I don't want to make new things* (F-48, lower). Or as another woman reported: *The children today are attracted to chocolate, ice-cream and the like. They go for the sweetness. The sweetness is heavier and it makes them happier. But they don't eat food properly anymore. They eat less traditional food. We tell them not to eat too unhealthy food, but they don't listen and then they get a cough and a cold* (R-14). Women try to live up to all of their offspring's expectations, even though it strains the budget: *All the family members and the neighbours are having non-veg. If we don't prepare it, the children will feel bad* (F-48, lower). Another woman admitted to be pressured by

---

[12] In addition to the here described new demands in the nutritional sector, the increase in childrens' stores for toys and cloths, observable for example on Himayatnagar main road are another clear indicator on what Hyderabad's aspirers tend to spend their money.

the demands of his son: *I'm worried about him, whenever he's here with us in the city. Because he needs non-veg and dal, vegetables and curd. He demands it, but I can't provide it daily, because it's too expensive. The children neither accept liquid dal. When I have to reduce the quantity, they complain, because they are used to the taste*. Further on, she made an interesting comment referring to her children's' capabilities: *I worry most about my children. They are not as daring and brave as we are, because they don't face the same problems* (Sikh-49). Therefore, *we pray to God to take care of our children. They are innocent and don't know about prices and all* (ibid.). Children clearly have the pole position. They are a reason to stop working, although the salary might be needed: *I used to work as a teacher, but stopped because of the kids. At the end of the month, it might get a little tight, but whatever the children need, I buy* (R-08). On the other hand, many women reported that their children sense when it gets tight and stop asking for extras: *My oldest daughter is very intelligent, she understands the family problems and never demands anything* (F-48, lower).

Hence, the most pressing parental concerns are the well-being of their children. In globalising Hyderabad, this means a good education to ensure a secure and well-paid job, which will also help the family as a whole: *Educating my children is most important to me. And then my son will help my husband with the business and we'll have two incomes* (R-29). *At least they have education. And they'll think of their younger siblings once they are settled in.* (F-48, lower) Thus, to enable good education for their offspring is a means of safeguarding the parents' own future. Furthermore, education is seen as an absolute necessity, because *there is so much competition now, everybody has to read. Kids don't have the freedom to play anymore. There are lots of pressures* (R-15). This can even weaken or break up traditional structures as is demonstrated by the re-evaluation of what a girl should have: *Our daughter should get well educated and settled. After that, we'll think of her marriage* (R-44). *Nowadays, education is also for girls important, so we spend more on education and less on the dowry* (R-15). *Her education is more important than her wedding. We can't know about her marriage life, it might be good or bad, but at least she should have a good education* (R-36).

Yet, education in India is, apart from government schools, not free of charge and every family seeks to send their children to good private schools. Thus, education was called *our biggest problem nowadays*, because *it's very expensive and we have to take loans* (R-26). Most women claimed that education is affordable as long as the kids are small, yet becomes more and more expensive: *I'm worried about my children's' education. My oldest now does the +2, so she needs books and good cloths, because they don't wear uniforms anymore*[13]. *I think of my children's' education, that it'll be interrupted when we are unable to pay the fees* (F-48, lower). Albeit this woman belonged to a lower class, her worries are shared by many.

Apart from a good school education, other values are not ignored and are considered to be just as important: *I want my children to study well, have a good life and that they should have good manners. Because even if they are in good health, a good position and wealth, with bad manners you get no respect in society and the family. Human values are very important* (R-31).

To sum up, it does not come as a surprise that the only time a perceived economic vulnerability appeared, was in relation with the children's education or, to a smaller, the daughter's marriage. Next to here described risk factors, an especially important and clearly cultural specific array of risks are those which are related to the family in general and to religious life.

5.3 Threats to the socio-cultural self

The Cultural Theory (see Chapter 1) points out that those hazards, which are identified as threats to local and socio-cultural values are rated as especially serious. In the world of here questioned women, three occasions activate risk behaviour: *We adjust after festivals, functions and visitors* (R-14). This can be explained with one of the highest regarded values in the Indian culture: The principle of 'Atithi Devo Bhava', of 'guest is God' (see Hofmann and Dittrich 2009) is strictly regarded by all respondents and ensures the social cohesion of extended families, neighbours and friends: *Sometimes we spend even more, when we have more family members at home. But if we see our relatives, we are happy. If it would be only me and my husband, it would be boring. We'll always share, it makes us happy. I grew up this way. Village people always came to our house, I grew up feeding others, even those who we didn't know.* (R-22). Yet, as this women indicated, serving others can also be a social burden, especially when the budget is tight: *When my first daughter got married, we had to take a loan for we hadn't saved enough money. Yet, when we have guests, we still serve them the thin rice and meat; we'll adjust for the rest of the days with sambar and rasam.*[14] *Everyone gives preference to the guests, it's like feeding God* (R-05). Thus, no one would risk their reputation by not complying with this principle: *For us, it is compulsory to serve our visitors. It's a sign of respect, we serve them and keep them happy* (R-13). Although *at the end of the month, it can*

---

[13] The 10+2 is required before entering higher education.
[14] Sambar is a dal-based, rasam a tomato-based soup.

get tough. For example, when we had a lot of family visiting (R-01). Keeping this in mind, the frank statement of one lower class woman becomes understandable: *For some visitors, we also spend more money, but it depends on the persons' importance* (R-07, lower).

Another source of extra-expenditures is religious festivals. An upper-class woman gives following interpretation: *I think we have so many festivals, because it is the only time we celebrate and treat ourselves with something special. Especially the families with a limited income would get special items only for festivals* (interview with Radha Reddy, 23.11.2009). Most families buy new cloths only for Dassara and/or Divali: *We have to buy them for the children, because everybody has new cloths* (R-35). They save extra money to prepare special treats for visitors and make sure that everything looks neat and clean: *During the festival times, I have a lot more work to do with all the cleaning and other preparations. I always worry a little that I don't have enough time, but the preparations are compulsory. Others will come during the festival season and ask, so I have to show my preparations. I receive special foods on festivals, so I also have to offer special food* (R-04). Here as well, the reputation is important and one woman, who otherwise is quite adventurous with food, confessed that *for functions and festivals I don't try the new recipies, it's too risky* (F-46).

During the course of the year, not only festivals are a time of family gatherings, at least as many, yet usually even more functions (i.e. weddings or other family festivities) are celebrated. While a wedding means new cloths and presents on the guests' side, the bride's family not only carries the burden of catering the festivities, they foremost have to provide dowry. Most parents start to save for it with the birth of a girl-child and *will never touch that money, not even for food* (R-01). Other families take out loans: *We adjusted due to the marriage of the first daughter. But we don't see it as a problem, because it's important that the daughters get good families. And we have a satisfaction that she's happy, so we are happy to adjust. Our son doesn't say anything either, he'll adjust. After paying off the loan, we'll change back again* (R-05). Some count on the family's assistance: *In our family, our girls need lots of jewellery for their marriages. In this perspective, I expect assistance from my son, but I'm worried, that he won't support us* (Sikh-49). Yet, some families also adjust their life cater a daughter in-law, for example: *Now, we plan for the construction of more rooms so we save as a chit. We also want other assets, because a girl will come and we need a certain standard. So it has to be done* (F-46). In this regard, it was interesting to observe that women whose offspring recently got married, noticeably had less to lament and claimed to be free of any tensions or worries.

Remains one last sector where cultural values lead to a specific risk behaviour, albeit included into the daily routine: eating habits contingent on religion. Fasting in the name of God is common and many people rejoice from meat at least one or two days a week: *We don't like it [meat, R.H.] more often, because on the other days, we fast and do pooja* (R-12). For pooja purposes, they also *make some special foods to offer to the deities* (R-22, higher). One interesting case emerged in the Sikh community, where the family re-evaluated their religious behaviour: *We fast on Fridays. We also used to fast on a full moon, but then we listened to the verses of our Holy Book and we thought: 'why to kill your soul through fasting? So we stopped now. Fasting troubles the soul, because it's hungry, so we can't do perfect prayers!* (R-49, Sikh)

In general, although some cultural practices peril the households' budget and savings and therefore expose the families to the risk of falling back to lower classes, they are widely accepted as cultural obligations. Next chapter will be on another aspect whose appreciation is crucial for the general and further understanding of Indian risk perception.

5.4 The trust and responsibility of things to come

One element of the risk concept is that it also serves to turn future events into something foreseeable and calculable (see Zwick & Renn 2002). This way, uncertainty becomes manageable, an instance used by insurance policies. Generally, our modern society regards future events no longer as unavoidable occurrences caused by God, they are rather "dealt with in an intellectual contemporary way with almost a moral obligation to shape the future according to one's wishes" (Zwick & Renn 2002: 1).

Yet, the Indian society, deeply rooted in world religions of Hinduism and Islam, demands a differentiated view of handling present and future for several reasons: The Hinduistic trait of reincarnation suggests an upwardly ambition with the sole focus and concern towards the next life. Therefore, Hindus are said to not care about the here and now, which is an important aspect in risk evaluation[15]. At the same time, the outcome of prospective events is left in God's hands, an attitude which is not restricted to the families' pooja rooms, but adheres to the society as a whole. For instance, mass prayers, announced in the newspaper, were held on November 28 in a sports stadium

---

[15] The severe implications of such a religious apathy are object of newer studies on ecological behaviour (Pandeya 1992; Chapman et al. 1997; Kremer 2004: 26).

to prevent natural calamities and ensure world peace and welfare for all living beings (Hindu, 25.11.2009b). A whole day dedicated to ensure a better future! The idea of a periodic future deriving from Hinduism, however, is crisscrossed by the belief in a lineal upwards trend. This foremost material optimism was launched by the liberalisation of the market and the subsequent economic boom starting from 1991, accompanied by a fast globalisation. However, this positive conviction, pushed by the fast economic growth, suffered severely with recent economic recession. This means, the generation growing up in the certitude that everything continuously changes for the better, suddenly is confronted with a desolate economy in which the investment in education is not necessarily rewarded with a good job: *My son took the test to become a government employee. But as so many participated, they raised the marks and so my son didn't get in, even though he had enough points according to the old scale. Why do they do that?* (F-47) It is characteristic for the middle classes to be a highly mobile group, making them fairly vulnerable, which is especially felt in connection with their children: *Still, I feel bad, because 50 % of whatever I enjoyed, I'm not able to give to my children. I feel very bad about this* (F-48, lower).

This also means that they are still connected with both worlds and move between the traditional yesterday and the modern tomorrow, resulting in an incredible flexibility and adaptive capacity. Disappointed by the secular modernity, however, the religion once more comes to the fore with a return to pre-modern values, also applied to material aspects. At the same time, dissatisfaction and a new perceived poverty spread out and this has to be seen as one possible reason for the increase of violent disruptions in recent years. Nevertheless, the disembodiment of risks from the individual, paired with their ascription to the religious sphere, also generates new optimism and offers one way to take care of the future, for example through the common habit of giving special offers in July *for our children's' bright future and health*[16] (F-48, lower class). The respondent further explained: *We leave things to God, we pray regularly. For example, yesterday was the end of the month after divali. My two older girls did pooja and prayed for their education. We offer a coconut every Monday, it's compulsory, but a little sugar for it is enough. At least we have to offer some things* (F-48, lower). This demonstrates various elements in the notion of present and future and thereby in the handling of threats:

---

[16] In July, Hyderabad celebrates the Bonalu festival, which marks the end of summer. Originally, Bonalu–a fat, dark skinned Goddess, usually depicted in anger and always erected outside the villages–was worshiped by those casts, which were not allowed in temples. Later, rural people offered sacrifices to ask for protection from cholera and the like. Over the time, Bonalu has become the Goddess who navigates the future (interview with research assistant Supriya).

1. The religious trust in God: *We leave it to God to reduce our stress.* (additional comment by research assistant Supriya),

2. paired with the acceptance of one's fate: *Whatever we have, we are happy with it* (R-25), and simultaneously

3. an optimistic glance towards a better future.

Of course, this has severe consequences on the rating of their own capacity to control the future: *Whatever will happen, we don't know, so how can we think about it?* (R-32) As a 'crisis-oriented' society, they tend not to think about possible damage events: *I didn't really think about the future yet* (R-30), until their occurrence and only then they react: *I only think about cutting back or other ways [to reduce stress, R.H.] when I have to* (R-21). This is valid for short-term thinking: *I plan only for the next day* (R-37), as well as for long-term planning: *As our daughter is still young, we'll save for her marriage in the future* (R-15). Aspects of our 'future-oriented' model of society only seem to rule when it comes to questions of the next generation: *With children, the future must be taken into consideration* (R-06). *The children should have a nice life with good education and good jobs. Otherwise, I don't have any thoughts about the future* (R-27). In fact, all hopes seem to be reflected towards the next generation: *Whatever we have, we like. But the children's' generation should have it better. They should get a good education and they should grow from where they are now. Now, it's ok to live, but if the prices still increase, they should have it better* (R-28). Yet, neglecting the days to come also carries the notion of being a simple necessity: *We don't think of tomorrow. We can't think of tomorrow, because we don't have any money* (Sikh-50, lower). And once in a while, even the devout lower class people struggle to accept their destiny: *Sometimes, we get angry with God. We do whatever we can, so why doesn't he bless us?* (F-48, lower) The time scale, again, has to be taken into consideration with latent risks, as they are not as easily delimitable as catastrophic events. At the same time, however, temporary food risks can induce long-term effects. If they are not tackled on spot, but dragged along, for example, due to adequate household management or misjudgement, severe nutritional consequences can occur.

As has become obvious, the Indian evaluation of things to come, hence the Indian concept of future bears consequences for the tolerance, valuation and mitigation of perceived risks. The lower middle class housewife hopes for a better future for her children and trusts in the fulfilment of her wishes with divine support. The importance of trust in the perception of risks is a basic element: *And one year ago, the goats and chicken had some disease, so now, we don't trust non-veg anymore. Before that incident, we had it a little more often. But we have less interest now* (R-40). Yet, trust is also an important determinant of how risks are perceived and dealt with, because trust is linked with responsibility (Zwick & Renn 2002: 44), which becomes clear in following statement: *But it all depends on God* (R-10). This impacts both the responsibility of situations and the evaluation of one's personal ability to change them accordingly: *The water and the air are polluted, yet, we are born into that world, what can we do about it? It's not in our hand* (R-44). The ruling conviction is that with living in a devout manner, as much as possible is done and everything else is not in their hands. This manner of pushing off responsibility has to be understood as inherent to the hierarchical Indian society and can also be observed in matters belonging to the profane world where, for example, the government has to take blame for most problems, albeit the national and local administration is not necessarily vested with the population's trust: *We can't change the government rules. Nowadays, everything is like that, what can we do?* (R-15), *[t]he costs of the products must be reduced. It's the Government's task, but it doesn't do it* (R-28).

The Cultural Theory predicates that attitudes towards risk vary according to cultural biases. Here, traits of the major category of 'hierarchists', who regard regulations and laws apt to monitor risk, became visible. Paul Slovic complemented the categories by a 'technological enthusiasm', which can be applied to the Indian attitude towards progress and modern technologies. Hence, trust plays an important role in the technology adoring, hierarchical society and will repeatedly be an important factor in the interpretation of various risks. Moreover, it should be evident by now that an emic approach to risk perception and valuation requires local and contextual categories.

5.5 The time factor

In these modern days, time has become a valuable commodity. Saving time is of upmost importance: *Women have less time nowadays. My husband and my children have to leave for work and college* (R-32). This concerns all aspects of the daily routine, be it shopping, *I don't have the time any more to go to the market, so I go to the nearby shop* (R-08), where time sometimes is perceived as more valuable than the costs themselves, *the shop might be costlier than the market, but it saves time* (R-23), or kitchen facilities. For example, fridges allow keeping vegetables for a couple of days and hence are seen as a great help, because *to go daily shopping takes time* (R-45). Electrical devices such as mixers and rice cookers are appreciated for various reasons: *I have a mixi and we got a rice cooker three or four months ago, because in the morning, we have to cook fast. A rice cooker is nice, because we only wash the rice and then it cooks by itself and meanwhile I can prepare the curries* (R-14). Another advantage stated was to need *less manual energy* to prepare chutneys and doughs (R-06). Thus, the possession of such kitchenware is in today's ever faster world perceived as almost necessary to handle the challenges of the daily routine. Table 4 shows the distribution of electronical kitchen devices in questioned households.

Table 4: Electronical devices in the households' kitchens

- Mixer 42 %
- Fridge 38 %
- Rice Cooker 20 %

Source: Own source and draft, 2009

However, financial security is not given in the lower middle class and households usually have to deal with a precarious economic position. This can eliminate the advantage of saving time, not only because there is not enough initial capital, but also because of consequential costs: *We don't have a fridge. It's too expensive and we would also have a higher current bill. We stay on rent, we can't use that much current. The owner then might say we use too much current* (R-44). Or: *We also have a rice cooker, but we only use it when there is no time. To use it more often, would increase the electrical bill* (R-33). That in nearly all households the TV is running most of the day is not reflected. In spite of financial difficulties, the feeling that such technological help is much needed is very strong: *We don't have a rice cooker, it's too expensive, but I would like to have one. It would save time and the children could prepare it themselves. A year ago, we bought the fridge. Since then, we go to the market weekly once for vegetables and they stay fresh. Before, we had to go daily or every two days. And we cook with gas, which is quicker, but therefore also less tasty* (R-15). The informant's last comment marks taste as the crucial point in traditional Indian food culture, which was repeatedly noted by the respondents, also in reference to time pressure which puts this value at risk and leads to following dilemma: *In the old days, we used to take to stone grinder and it was so tasty! With the electric one, the food is closed off from the air and it's not a slow grinding. But now we have less time. People go to office for work and everything has to be made fast* (R-25). Therefore, some women *still prefer the grinder. The chutneys in the stone grinder have a better taste and stay fresh for a longer time* (R-26).

Why chutneys this way should stay fresh for a longer time could not be explained by her, but she stressed that freshness is one important category of food. Nevertheless, in order to save time, some women would act in opposition to this still prevalent traditional value which also exemplifies the gravity of current societal changes and one woman admitted: *I'd also like a microwave, but it's too expensive. With a microwave, I could reheat food for the evenings and wouldn't have to cook twice* (R-19). The Indian technological enthusiasm, here, certainly also plays a role and technologies are believed to be a convenient risk manager. Yet, while the worry about time is omnipresent, most women resort to less costly options. Two of them explained: *Sometimes, I make bambino, if there is less time. If I have the time, I make chapatti. But only chapatti is not sufficient, you also need a curry. With bambino, you don't need an extra curry* (R-36). *To make daily tiffins is difficult with the child. So I feed him milk, bread and Maggi* (R-34). Costs and especially time are two very important factors in the women's risk assessment. Interestingly, this is also the case in households where the woman is not working or where she even has the support of a maid! It nearly appears as to be busy has turned into a cultural value. However, this has not happened without the modernity's downside, the increase of an overall pressure on the individual as well as on the society. A sad evidence are the "39 suicides a day in AP" (Sudhakar Reddy; DC, 18.11.2009a), which mostly occur among students and IT workers, who no longer can handle the ever increasing competition.

Following the discussion of time as a scarce resource, the respondents herein also saw one reason for the diminution in food quality: *The soil and everything is not natural anymore. They use chemicals to get more quantity in less time* (R-26). Chemicals in food are a heavily discussed subject (also see Hofmann 2009) and were mentioned in relation with almost every aspect as will become evident further down. To better understand the full scope of it, some information on the Indian food culture and eating habits are given before describing the perceived risks connected with food.

5.6 Exposure to risks of food and nutrition

5.6.1 Eating habits

In ancient India, what, when and with whom to eat has been subject to social and religious conditions and restrictions, according to one's class and caste. The priest caste of Brahmins, for example, had strict rules on pure foods and preparations and tried to avoid the risk of being touched by any lower caste member. This means that outsiders were not allowed in their kitchens, food was only taken after a bath, guests were served on disposable plates, etc. Adherence to regular meal timings, to categories of hot and cold food, and the observance of religious fasting as well as feasting days was common among most people.

Some traditional habits are still present, yet not easy to follow. For example, office hours in the large IT sector are often adjusted to serve American and European office hours, which means night-shifts for Indian workers. This is simply not compatible with principles such as *eating in timings* (R-02), although most respondents gave following definition of hunger: *You get hungry, when you don't eat timely* (R-03).

In the Indian context, whether or not a household eats animal products and is thus a non-veg family, depends mostly on religious affiliations, but can also have other reasons in relation with perceived risks which can either refer to its preparation: *Vegetables need less cleansing than non-veg* (F-46), or to social aspects as one mother said in reference to her daughter's veg-diet: *In school, most of her friends are Brahmins, so she was worried about eating meat* (R-22) In most lower class non-veg families, the preparation of meat is restricted to Sundays and maybe one other day. The here ruling economical factor, however, was admitted very reluctant and only after further questioning: *We are a non-veg family, but we only make it once a week. Not more often, because we don't like it that much (...). If we have money, than we buy mutton* (R-07). Re-directing and re-evaluating the chain of arguments was also observed with leafy vegetables, which were named especially healthy, maybe because they are also the cheapest.

In general, women had following attitude: *I cook traditionally, because I'm habituated to it* (R-18). *Yet, things are changing. Now, we have more dishes and we can vary according to our preferences. Before, we didn't have a choice. If we are hungry now, we have some snacks. Earlier, we only had cooked rice in the morning and had it till night* (R-32). This is not only a clear indicator of the on-going change, but also characterises once more the income group of the aspirers, caught between traditions and new allurements.

Yet, although some new products, for example Maggi noodles and certain ready-made sauces, were easily integrated in the kitchen and are not even perceived as new components, other traditional values still prevail. Freshness and pureness in the Indian context are not only indicators for good quality, but beyond that are also important cultural principles: *Even if there is not a lot of money, I adjust, so that I can buy the good quality things* (R-02). This need is very strong and with some responses it is not quite clear if they simply find suitable excuses for not being able to draw level with the others or if they actually are not subject to above described technological enthusiasm: *We don't have a fridge, because we don't like to use it, food will not stay fresh in there. And we only eat fresh things, even if it's costlier, it has to be fresh* (R-10, lower). The same can be said for taste, because *Taste goes over everything!* (R-31) In fact, many respondents rather refrain from convenience or lower costs: *I also have a rice cooker, but only use it in emergencies. We cook our daily rice on gas. If the rice in the rice cooker cools, it becomes stiff and has a different taste* (R-25). Members of the Sikh community are usually from the Panjab, a region in the North where people prefer wheat chapatti over rice, which is evident in this statement: *We get the rice from the ration shop. Yet, we won't cook it as rice. We'll prepare dosa and murkullu with it. When it is urgent, we'll also cook it, otherwise we don't like the taste* (Sikh-50, lower). They see the taste as lost for good, a loss, which weighs even more in reference to their children, as one lady showed with this annihilating judgement: *No matter how nicely we cook, it's not that tasty, we lost that kind of taste. We used to make rice with green chilli powder and it was very tasty. Today, it's not tasty anymore. The chemicals are in everything today and it has a different smell. Our children don't even know the real taste anymore. At least, we had better food, the next generation will have totally chemicalised food* (R-14).

5.6.2 Food adulteration

The three mentioned categories–freshness, purity and taste–are also the driving factors of the dominant disregard of ready-made and instant food[17]: *I only do the home-cooking, because I want to prepare everything fresh. And we mix things in the proper way, so it's energetic. For example, in the dosa batter, we use more pulses than rawa [semonlina]. With instant food, we don't know when they pack it. We care a lot about quality. For example, there are different prices for different qualities in apples. But if the quality of a high priced apple is not good, we don't buy it* (R-29). For most informants, low

---

[17] However, sauces and some seasoning mixes do not fall into this category and neither are considered ready-made foods.

quality, bad taste and the chemicals used are the main reasons to abstain from such products. Yet, while convenience usually comes over health, the higher costs certainly are a convincing factor to refrain from instant food. It is interesting to listen, on what kind of information the respondents base their judgement: *We don't use any instant foods and have never tried it. We heard from our neighbours that it can have worms and stones in it. It's of very low quality* (R-27). In general, the fact that the component of the unknown is fairly high with instant and ready-made products leads to a higher degree of uncertainty and only little control over the ingredients, which are both important factors of risk evaluation. The fear of food adulteration in the city is based on the same criteria, especially in connection with quality. Women with a rural background claim to refrain from buying certain stocks as they are adulterated with other grains or stones. Another woman gives much importance to a healthy diet and explained: *We also have laddu made with smashed dates and sesame, fried without any oil. We have that instead of milk, because they are full of calcium and packet milk might not be that pure. The fruits, for example, are waxed and the bananas have chemicals, but if we eat generally healthy, it's ok.* (R-20). In opposition to the western culture, where healthy food is often equated with a bitter or no taste, the Indian consumer regards health and taste as interdependent at least in reference to the traditional cuisine: *Fridge food tastes stale and my husband doesn't like it. It's also a health issue, because the nutrients may die in the fridge* (R-08).

One woman provided a summary of the so far discussed issues: *Foods today are not as tasty anymore. They use insecticides to preserve them for more days. For example, the tomato used to be smaller and had a slightly bitter and sour taste. Now it's big and sweet, because it's a hybrid. It also used to take less time to become a paste, now you have to cook it longer. They use chemicals to grow more* (R-13). The stigma of chemicalised food is also the leading topic, when it comes to the foods' origin and health.

5.6.3 Urban and rural agriculture

They use the chemicals, because people want to do less hard work, but want more money. It's easier to maintain the fields and grow the crops with chemicals. Everybody in the society knows that (R-44). Here, the distribution and balance of benefits and costs is perceived as unfair which makes the risk intolerable. Yet, a crucial difference is made between commercial agriculture and the way their rural relatives grow food: *When someone goes back to the village, he will bring back vegetables with less chemicals and good taste. But they grow very slow. I know if the vegetables are from the village or from the city by the smell and the shape of them. For example, the water in the city is polluted and you can see it on the stem of the leaves, it looks and smells different* (R-04). This can have a relevant influence on people's shopping behaviour, as *the vegetables from the market are from the village. The vegetables of the bandis [push-cart of street food vendors] are city vegetables and therefore not healthy* (R-01). Yet, even if vegetables and fruits are grown in a 'natural' way, the distance they have to travel and the time of storage until they reach the final consumer is regarded as a threat to their freshness. Women, even those originating from the city, agree that *[r]ural people are stronger, they do more hard work and eat very good food. We have the vegetables in the village, so we cut them when we want them. In the city, you only get them after they have been exchanged through many hands* (R-41).

Another problem is water quality, which of course is attributed to chemicals: *We filter our water, because the company that supplies our water uses chemicals in it as the pipes are so bad* (R-26). Yet, most people complain about muddy water, especially during the rains of the monsoon season. Polluted water and ingredients are the reasons why outside food (restaurants excluded), often equated with junk food, is rejected by many: *Generally, outside food is less hygienic, they use low quality oil and low quality products* (R-02). In addition, *uncovered prepared food from outside is unhealthy because of the dust and water* (R-16). *They also serve previous food, which may not be fresh* (R-23). Again, freshness and purity determine the evaluation of outside food. Nevertheless, in spite of this stigmatisation, taste cannot be ignored and most women said that their children are crazy for it. With above mentioned doubts about the health aspect, however, the informants, as responsible mothers, try to keep the consumption of street food as low as possible, even though it means extra work: *But the children don't listen, they bring it at any cost. When I don't prepare any of it, they'll get it from outside, so I start to prepare the snacks again* (R-18).

Last but not least, another reason to restrain from outside food is the higher cost of it: *As we don't have any stability with our business, we don't want to take the risk of spending money on outside food* (R-12).

5.7 Health at risk

In general, the traditional idea of a healthy body and soul is based on a balanced diet of 'hot' and 'cold' foods. Thus, food and health are directly interlinked and fragments of this ancient wisdom linger on, yet also lead to many misconceptions when mixed with newer ideas. For example, people see in the consumption of potatoes and *brinjal* (eggplant) the cause of joint pains or claim eating tomatoes in combination with leafy vegetables of generating kidney stones. A healthy body, however, is an important asset of lower classes (see Chamber 1989: 4) and resembles the foundation of a secure future, which is why ruling health concepts are foremost directed towards children: *The children should get settled and they should be healthy so they can do their work. I should be healthy, too, because if I'm healthy, I can take care of my children* (R-29). Mothers prepare whatever they consider good for their offspring: *I don't eat fish, but prepare it for my children. I don't like the smell, but we should still have it for the children's' sake* (R-14). With the TV as the housewives' main companion, the majority of the respondents even consider Maggi noodles as being *highly protenised and vitaminised* (R-30, higher). The contribution to one's health is also judged according to own observations, for example: *Whenever the children ask for it, I'll prepare Maggi. It's healthy, I know that, because the children eat it and stay healthy* (R-19). Thus, *if anything is unhealthy, we see the results and we'll stop eating it* (R-36). In this context, to follow certain rules automatically guarantees a healthy living: *We have fruits twice a week. We buy them from bandis, they are nice quality. Apart from that, we eat vegetables, non-veg, mainly egg and leafy vegetables. So our family is healthy* (R-07). Some products, such as Horlicks and other milk powders are simply judged healthy, because they are sold at pharmacies. One woman further explained: *In the old days, we were not health conscious, but today women work and are health conscious* (R-29).

Regarding the society as a whole, heart attacks and cancer were named the biggest health challenges. In reference hereto, people agreed that *[o]besity is the foundation of diseases* (R-31). Overweight and diabetes are especially prevalent in urban Andhra Pradesh and therefore also in the local mind-set: *Our problem is that we all do sedentary work. The normal diet is no problem for hard workers, but we can't digest it anymore, because we mostly sit* (R-20). This was also the opinion of another lady, who, albeit being fairly skinny, nevertheless took up a diet: *I do the diet, because I don't want to become fat. I started it three years ago for beauty and health reasons. That's also why I don't have a maid. I want to do the physical work* (R-10, lower). Not having a maid for this reason was indeed named by various women. To sum up, a nutritionist explained: *We are not a nutrition based country, we are just traditional eaters. We never controlled the quantity of what we ate, but we had a higher physical activity. Only now, we introduce the concept of quantity and quality* (Interview with Radha Reddy, 23.11.2009)[18]

---

[18] For further information on the awareness of diabetis and obesity, also see Hofmann and Dittrich 2009.

5.8 Shopping behaviour

I see the different qualities and prices, I compare and then I buy (R-29). As seen above, variety and quality, in addition with economic aspects are defining criteria for food in general, in which the acquisition of food has to be included. Thus, the choice of shopping locations is dependent on these aspects. Most of the informants *prefer the market, because it has more quantity, better quality and lower costs* (R-06), and *never go to the supermarket, unless in urgent occasions or if it's on the way. They have fixed prices there and you can't trade like on the wholesale market. You only safe money when you buy on bulk, otherwise there are too many fluctuations* (R-02).

Yet, to analyse where people get their groceries is a good example of how perceptions can vary: *I walk to the Mahalaxmi supermarket, because it's hygienic and neat. They clean the dust and you get good rates. They have price tags. If the vendor of the village-grown vegetables is available somewhere, I will prefer him* (R-04). While this woman still rather buys village vegetables, another respondent has completely changed her preferred location: *I go to Reliance Fresh because they have reasonable rates and it's fresh. Before that, I have only gone to the market, but the market is even more expensive than the supermarket. To the supermarket, I go between four and five p.m., because then they have the fresh stock* (R-03).

While most people agree that products at the supermarket are cleaned, yet more expensive, street food vendors, so called bandis are the lowest in the opinion: *The rythu has good food compared to bandis. I go to those vendors who have the food from the villages and where the weighing is good* (F-48, lower). Only *veggies and fruits you can buy from the bandis, because you can clean them at home* (R-16). Given the omnipresent smell of excrement and the garbage on the streets, the tag of dirt and health risk is not very astonishing.

They had a similar low opinion on kiranas, the local mom-and-pop stores. Most people claim to go there only in emergencies as the kirana usually charges more for products of lower quality. Yet, some households argue: *The costs level out as to go by two-wheeler is expensive compared to the higher prices at the kirana. For me, the time aspect is most important* (R-21). Other families who cannot afford to buy in bulk also rely on the small kiranas, which are never far away as the high density of the Tilak Nagar map perfectly demonstrates.

Although the majority of the respondents made a point in choosing the cheapest merchant, in fact, they do not actually compare the rates with other places. Thus, another factor must play a crucial role in the choice of shopping locations, which has

Figure 11: l: Street food vendor in Tilak Nagar. r: Man at fruit bandi in Saroor Nagar.
Source: Own source, Oct/ Nov 2009

importance in evaluating processes and was already mentioned: trust. In this case, trust in food authorities, merchants and salespersons. The vast majority of the interviewees have, over the years, established a trust relationship with vendors, who sold them good quality products at fair rates: *But I prefer to get everything from the same shop, because as a regular client we get better quality and a better price* (F-47) In a culture where bribery is a daily occurrence, face-to-face relationships are given a particular priority, especially on the background of food adulteration and the like. This generates an overall notion of mistrust, which is further fuelled by media reports such as on businesses, which allegedly sell ghee adulterated with fat of dead cattle to hotels and restaurants. As usually the check post often is taking bribes, such business usually continues unchecked (DC, 20.10.2009). Trust relationships can have a long history and often have their roots in village or family structures: *Yearly, we get rice from the Nalgonda district. We know some people there, so we get good quality rice. Here in town, it's mixed with other things* (R-14). This goes so far that people, who moved within the city, often go back to their old neighbourhood to purchase staples from their trusted businesses.

All respondents follow an interesting shopping pattern: *Every two or three days we go to the nearby market. If we had a fridge, we would get vegetables once a week. My husband gets fruits on his way home from office, rice, turmeric and chilli powder we get once a year. Everything else once a month, when the salary comes* (R-40).

Various factors help to keep the costs low, for example buying it crude, in bulk, from relatives or after the January harvest, when *everything is cheaper* (R-11). The same women further explained: *To get it monthly, it's too difficult as we have other things to buy monthly.* Yet, saving money through buying in bulk is only possible for those who dispose of a relatively large amount of it at the beginning of the year. Others cannot afford this one-time investment: *Every four to five months, we get dal and rice at a very near place with the two-wheeler. We don't buy it yearly, because we don't have the money* (R-18). Apart from managing the finances, problems with storage and processing dictate the shopping behaviour: *We have to get it monthly, because for longer it won't stay fresh and undamaged* (R-10, lower), or: *Monthly, we buy dal. The processing like drying it outside would be too much hassle when buying it yearly* (R-22).

It has become clear that certain factors are relevant for the perception and evaluation of threats and risks. The role of trust has been discussed sufficiently. One more factor, voluntariness has been mentioned. For the evaluation of risks, it makes a great difference if they are taken voluntarily or not. For example, natural risks are usually perceived as unavoidable and hence involuntary and uncontrollable. Some of the risks mentioned during the interviews can be traced back to human action, such as genetically modified food, food adulteration and, to a certain extent also increasing food prices. Hence, they are theoretically avoidable and consequently more likely to be judged negative.

5.9 Increase in food prices

Most women mentioned the increasing prices: *One year ago, we spent a lot less. It's compulsory to have dal on Saturday, that's a costly affair as we need one cage [one kg, R.H.] for one meal* (F-47), and while speaking about it, they gathered more and more momentum. While at first glance it seemed as though they acquiesce to it, once brought up, they indeed had a lot to say. When it comes to their diet, *everything is compulsory* (R-27): *For us, it's compulsory to have food, right? Even with less money* (R-19). Again, the worry about children leads to a stronger risk evaluation: *I can't compromise with food, because the children should have nutritious food in their growing state* (R-31). Yet, it later turned out that they apply a multitude of tricks and strategies to save money on food: *I used to make dal on alternate days, now I make it twice a week. Before, I prepared two kg per week, now it's two kg per month!* (F-48, lower) The importance of the traditional diet has been noted earlier and cutting it back as reported by this informant carries the notion of a perceived risk to food security, at least in terms of the population's food sovereignty as defined by the FAO. Moreover, higher prices pose a threat mostly in combination with other costs, especially those which are necessary to pay for the above discussed values such as education, marriage, festivals and visitors: *Of course, I'm worried about it, especially with the education fees also increased* (R-27). This often leads to a double or even multiplied burden for the household: *Every cost* has increased, so we cut on cloths and going out. When our daughter got married nine months ago, it was tight. Before, we also had the daughter's income, but she's gone now. Since our daughter is married, her family members will stop by. To serve them properly, we cut on mutton and give it to the family when they come for a visit (R-40).

The symbolic power of such cultural values has found a new level with growing financial assets and some of the women who are not yet at such a level actually blame the newly rich for rising prices: *People who have money spend more on functions now, that also makes prices go up* (R-44). When talking about prices, economic assets of the household evidently make a difference and less well-situated families struggle to make ends meet. Albeit lower middle classes are officially not eligible for ration-cards, some families are in possession of one. When buying at government fair-price shops, however, they come up with a whole elegy: *The dal, which we get at the ration-shop, doesn't cook right and it even gives gas to the body. It has stones mixed in it. The dal is not cooked even after more time. Due to the price hike, the government gives toor dal at the ration-shop, but it is in such bad quality. Previously, we only got rice, wheat and kerosene. We get ? kg dal for each family in a month. That's not even enough for one time. It's not much, but still we have to accept it. As the prices are high, the dealer is forcing us to take the dal. He says that only if we take the dal and wheat, do we get rice and kerosene. No one wants to buy dal of bad quality, not even we, so they are forcing us* (F-46).[19] This clearly shows that they are not even aware of their rights and possibilities to complain such unrightful treatment and instead they say: *We can't talk to the dealer, because he shouts at us that it is up to the government and what it supplies. In the fair-price shop, they don't give us as the correct amounts. I feel like fighting in the fair-price shop, but I'm afraid that he'll be angry and reduce our amounts. My oldest daughter, however, fights a lot with him, but it doesn't help* (F-48, lower).

All families adjust in one way or the other, albeit it sometimes means an extra burden: *If I had enough money, I would go to the wholesale once a month, but now I have to buy more in kiranas, where it is costlier, but where you can buy in less quantity* (R-05). Being forced to buy at kiranas was not easily admitted by the respondents due to the stigma of low quality products sold.

When it comes to prices, people feel helpless and while some name the increasing demand and new availability, *[c]osts have doubled, because the seasons have changed,*

---

[19] One women of the Sikh community, which traditionally prefers wheat over rice, made an interesting declaration on their special way of dealing with bad quality: *Sometimes, we have a ration-card, but our children don't like the rice. So we get it for Rs. two, sell it for ten and buy the Rs. 35 rice at the market.* (Sikh-49)

for example, we get mangos now, but it's not the season (R-27), some blame it on the government: *The government should stop the black market which holds back things and makes them more expensive* (F-46). Others again mention the growth of population or see higher forces acting: *Seasons are changing and even the winter is warmer. I don't know why, but seasons are less reliable. It's due to outside reasons and we can't do anything about it* (R-14). Of course, the severe floods of 2009 are also in the local population's mind: *The price rise is caused by the floods. The fields don't get watered properly. At the time of growing, there are no rains and during harvest time, there are floods. So we have big losses there. From the past one or two years, unseasonal things are happening. This month, we should grow rice, but there are no rains. I don't know why. It's nature, it's not in our hands. Yet, we should think positive, maybe it changes again. If not, there will be a shortage of everything. In this case, whatever we have, we eat. And when there is a problem, we eat less. Villagers adjust, but here in the city, no one wants to adjust. Everyone wants tasty food* (R-39). The words of this woman nicely exemplify all so-far made observations. Although higher prices due to monsoon floods are a common occurrence, the perception in 2009 seems to be extraordinary strong and it is interesting to note that many women mention in this regard the change in seasons. This could either be generated by actual observances or by the intensified media attention on climate change.

Nevertheless, it lies in the human nature to look for someone to blame and in this case, once again, merchants and the government are an easy prey: *If the farmers have less production, it's not the problem. The merchants have enough stock. They make the public suffer! And that we have higher prices now, it's the Government's fault, because we have to pay for the flood victims* (Sikh-49). In this woman's perception, costs and benefits are distributed unequally, causing her evaluation of being treated unfair.

To sum up, for households with an average income of Rs. 14,500, the price increase does not yet pose a serious threat, although they already spend about a third of their income on food (yearly provision of rice and chillies excluded). Moreover, higher prices are not unusual for this time of the year and the media reports are promising: "Food prices will fall by March, says Montek" (DC, 09.11.2009). In addition, most people still live off their yearly supplies: *We bought the rice before the price increased, so we don't have to think about it, but it's compulsory that we have the stored rice* (R-03). Yet, what about buying the yearly supplies for 2010? In reference to prices, most women have the foresight to worry about their existence in a long-term perspective, especially with the double-burden of other prices increasing simultaneously, for example the costs of education. Therefore, the respondents do not necessarily ask for lower cost, but rather hopes for higher salaries. The question if lower middle classes are at the stake of becoming more vulnerable or if their savings will be enough to buffer the increased expenditures of the daily diet is discussed in the following.

5.10 The risk of being vulnerable

The reality of lower middle classes is that they *don't really have any chances for adjustments, as we don't spend our money lavishly* (R-31). Food prices, rents and school fees are constantly rising, yet people either do not have any savings or had to use them up with no space to accrue new savings: *Earlier, we used to save some money, now we have to spend it all. In case of emergencies, we won't have any money. We don't have any savings, but we can't cut on anything either.* (R-15) Indeed, instead of the economic progress to which most of the respondents are used, the budget has become tighter. One woman confirmed: *Two years ago, I bought a fridge. I saved the money for it and bought it in monthly rates. Back then, it was not that difficult, today I couldn't manage* (R-24). While lower middle class households are in a general struggle to keep up with the increasing costs of living, saving money or paying back loans, becomes an extra burden which leads to a particular vulnerability. This is often severed by cultural requirements: *We don't have any problems with the cut backs, but now we have to start saving for the second daughter's marriage* (R-05). Has the family more than one daughter, this can lead to severe economic stress: *When our first daughter got married, we had to sell the house, so now I'm worried about my two other daughters. We totally depend on our business* (R-12). Thus, the basic vulnerability of lower middle classes can be either aggravated through extra, however cultural-immanent expenses such as visitors and marriages, or cause a serious threat to the household when it is hit by extraordinary costs. As one woman explained: *When my son fell from the first floor, he needed surgery. For that, I had to sell our field in the village, which we had gotten from my mother-in law after the wedding. I felt very bad about it. But I have another plot, too. It's good, because we should give property to our children. My income from the block is put apart for my daughters' marriages. If the families to-be want more, I'll have to ask for loans* (R-24). Families of this economic level hardly spend their money on unnecessary things and following statement is far from meaning lavish expenditures: *If we have any extra money, we spend more, for example on cloths* (R-16). When they say, *first come health and good food. Then we can think about saving* (R-22), it means that they try to sustain a basic standard and not any extravagances. Nevertheless, the Indian optimism surfaces here as well and many families are confident to be able to stock up their savings in the near future.

5.11 Influences on perceptions

Wishes and standards, as well as behaviour are subject to various influences. They for example depend on the peoples' origin: *I'm from the village, so I don't prepare Maggi. Yet, I'm habituated to the life in the city. I can't do heavy work anymore. But I would prefer to live in the village. Everything there is free and from our own field. Here, we have to buy everything! Only if we work we get food, in the village you get it even without work!* (R-41) In general, however, lower middle classes are aspirers with new demands, often dictated by the media: *By watching TV, we changed a lot. We want different things now* (R-32). Households seek to be on level with neighbours and friends: *We bought the fridge, because the surrounding families have one* (R-43). Children, of course, also have a strong voice and parents try everything to fulfil their wishes. In addition, women are liable to their mothers and mothers in-law and comply with their husbands' instructions: *We got a rice-cooker and a mixi gifted, but I don't use them. My husband says we shouldn't use them. I have to use the grinder; I'm not even allowed to use the pressure cooker!* (F-47) They also listen to neighbours and their doctors, yet, *the media plays a very big role in the awareness process. It educates people which are not literate* (R-31). In relation to health, the media not only broadcasts a whole glut of advices, but has engendered the perception and awareness of personal and societal health risks in the first place: *Now, health problems are broadcasted in TV, so people take better care of their health. These health programmes started recently. Earlier, nobody was interested, but now the health problems have increased* (R-31). Other issues are also pushed by the media, this way contributing to the knowledge-creation and raising the awareness of relevant topics such as climate change, which leads to a complex dynamic of risk perception. The media also leads to the processing of seemingly disconnected and fragmentary information, which is often a reason for uncertain or wrong evaluations. One woman, for example, explained: *The floods are causing the high prices. The floods in Kurnool have smashed the fields. This is all due to unseasonal days, the summer is lasting more days, the rain comes late. We have unseasonal climate due to pollution and the cutting of trees. So everyone should plant trees and reduce the pollution. If nothing is done, the heat will increase a lot and we'll get many diseases and less food production* (R-29).

Last but not least, cultural habits have a definite significance and exert great influence of which following statement gives proof: *We don't like to have cold food or water, but our family has grown now and many members will come and ask for cold water* (R-32).

In the same way, any behaviour aimed at coping with stress and risks has to be analysed with regard to the people's social, economic and cultural living conditions.

5.12 Adaptive capacities and mitigation behaviour

The perception and evaluation of risks are subject to certain risk characteristics, some of which have already been addressed, for example the factor of voluntariness. A similar role plays whether or not risks are estimated as influenceable, hence manageable or at least to some extent controllable. In the case of urban India, people feel helpless in many ways: *Even though it is the government's fault, we just have to adjust* (R-06), and the degree of resignation is high: *I can't do anything about it* (R-27). This is also valid for chemicalised food, because people do not know about alternatives such as organic farming or dismiss it as impossible with the air and water so heavily polluted. Outside food, on the other hand, can be avoided and is therefore controllable. A person with sufficient self-confidence is likely to have a positive attitude towards those risks, which he identifies as controllable by him. Yet, when the control (as a notion of trust) over most aspects in life is transferred to God or government agencies, the factor of personal control has less power and applies to only some areas.

Referring to initially elucidated vulnerability, Chambers (1989) links internal coping capabilities on a local level with external threats and hazards and refers to this interplay as a society's vulnerability. He concludes that particularly the most vulnerable people respond in a diverse and creative manner to risks (see Bohle & Glade 2008: 101). Albeit the here studied income group is certainly not the most vulnerable group, they nevertheless show a creative and flexible coping behaviour. However, if people believe that one's personal destiny is determined by faith and fate, the urge of own action is rather unincisive: *I'm happy with whatever I have and I pray that it will continue like this* (R-24). Thus, mitigation strategies are not necessarily aimed at fighting the root of threats, but are small-scale behavioural adaptations to risk situations: *We don't think about the future, only when it comes that far* (R-37). In addition, most households hardly have the financial means to put aside a monthly amount: *We first think of the daily things and we'll buy only important things* (R-18). Exceptions are children: *For our girls' marriages we started saving in time* (R-14), and occasions of high cultural value: *I also take from our savings for festivals and functions* (R-21). The most common saving scheme is a life insurance, usually 'a LIC' (Life Insurance Corporation of India). Many families also have plots in their or their children's names; some women are also a member of small-scale local saving groups, usually initiated by a social worker. *Short term savings with financing people* (R-19) are rare and credits are usually only given to house owners. Health insurance is also less common, unless the employer pays for it, which is a great advantage of government jobs, seeming to ease life in general: *As my husband is a government employee, we don't have any worries* (F-47). In addition to benefits, government jobs also mean secured income, an important aspect in the women's evaluation of their life situations: *I'm happy with my husband's salary, but not with my sons'. It's not secure as they work for private companies and not for the Government* (R-24).

Apart from taking official loans, most families rather resort to their relatives who offer better conditions: *We got the loan from family members, we have to pay it off now, but at least we don't have to pay any interests as with financing schemes* (R-40). Most families live within the surroundings of their relatives and have close relations with them. This allows a general reciprocity and ensures that no word of financial shortages reaches the neighbours: *We got some loans from family members and we still ask them when we are in need. They live nearby and we give back everything the next time. We don't like taking anything from others* (R-07). Safeguarding the family's reputation is the ultimate ambition. Nevertheless, the opposite case, where women would rather ask friends for help than family members also exists, yet some again have made bad experiences with both options: *I don't want any help from friends or relatives. That only creates problems* (R-24). Nevertheless, social capital, in the sense of "social networks and the norms of reciprocity associated with them" (Putnam 2002: 3) is, albeit not always recognised as such, an important contribution to the people's "asset portfolio management" (Moser 1998: 14; cited in: Noe 2007: 38).

In general, families put aside a little money whenever they have the possibility: *If we have more money, I don't want to spend all of it, I want to save some for another time* (R-18). This 'other time' usually means festivals and functions or family visiting. If households cannot resort to a financial cushion, they *have to adjust at the end of the month. Visitors would still get the same food; we have to cut the costs on other things, because food comes first* (R-02). The women keep the costs low in various ways, the most basic is to *make sure that there won't be left-overs* (R-27), which previously have been thrown out or given to the maid.[20] Outside food, together with the consumption of meat and fruits are usually reduced first, because they are comparatively expensive. Moreover, preparation practices, *we make dal with more water and eat thick rice* (R-06) as well as eating behaviour, *[w]e used to have dal every other day, now we only have it twice a month* (R-42) are adjusted. Yet, as said before, to "cut on vegetables and eat dal sambar" (R-08) means to jeopardise the families' nutrition and health as the nutritionist Radha Reddy explained. Most women therefore resort to cheaper products, for example to other varieties of dal or leafy vegetables to buffer their budget or they manage with careful planning: *We substitute curries with these things [spices with dal flour, soup with dried chillies, R.H.] once a week or once a month* (F-46). *Plus, if we prepare a costly vegetable, we can only have it once a day and then have a cheaper vegetable for dinner* (R-29). Most women saw the food inflation as a temporary crisis which did not worry them too much, especially as above discussed options still leave them some scope. All interviewees try to keep up a certain diet for their children, and parents forego their intake of fruits and tiffins in favour of them. The most startling comment in the rice eating south of India was following: *If the costs of rice further increase, we'll have rice once and then chapatti alternatively* (R-36).

In addition to altering the diet and recipies, people also adjust their shopping behaviour. Depending on their financial situation, they buy in bulk or *buy according to how much money there is daily or weekly. We only buy at kiranas, because we don't have the money for the supermarket. We adjust our expenses on food depending on the income* (R-12). Whenever peoples' living conditions include outside space and sufficient storing facilities, women resort to processing main ingredients at home, for example chilli powder, turmeric and dosa flour. This way, *there will be no adulteration and it's even of less cost. If you buy new rice, it's cheaper, you store it and then after two or three months, it increased in quantity and after six months, it has a good taste* (R-03). Furthermore, many families still have relatives in rural areas who live off their agricultural output and are thus an important source of basic staples: *Once a year we get rice, turmeric, dal and tamarind from the village. My mother has a field, but we still pay for it. However, it will be cheaper, fresh and of good quality. We go there during the festival season or for the summer holidays and bring it back with us* (R-19). With regard to the households' resilience,

---

[20] This, however, means one mitigation strategy less for the maids' families who often rely on such left-overs to secure three meals a day!

> *[t]he importance of keeping a rural economic base over large distances and long periods must not be underestimated in the context of material safety within a commodified, commercialised and monetarised urban sphere of life* (Krüger 2000: 54).

Social capital turned out to be a crucial determinator of the women's risk evaluation as it takes some of the dread with which other women are facing the rise in prices. The span of such social capital reaches far, one woman declared for example: *Nowadays, I have to spend more money on food, but I'm not worried, because I have three sons* (R-03). She is clearly thinking about the prospective dowries of future daughters in-law. On the other side, families whose daughters have already married pointed out to have one eater less! When speaking about family constellations, women also mentioned the pros and cons of joint families. While some argue that it enables the members to *adjust the money if one is not earning well* (F-46), others split up again and are happy not to have to spend as much money on meat and vegetables anymore.[21]

As described above, offering guests food and drink is compulsory in the Indian society, yet burdens the families' tight budgets. Nevertheless, hardly anyone would risk to loose face by declining this habit and this way dismissing the culture-immanent general reciprocity. However, some women made a discreet point in admitting to keep these expenditures as low as possible. In the words of one woman: *We still maintain relationships in a good way, but I don't spend much on them. I only invite the very important people and I seldom go to others' houses* (R-44).

Apart from the socio-cultural field, other applicatory coping strategies were listed by one housewife: *As the costs now have increased, we cut on different things. We only have one daily paper now where we used to have two. We buy fewer saris and less phone recharging cards. At festival and function time, I have my family members around from which I could borrow. Or we celebrate them combined* (R-23). Even though new cloths on certain festivals carry important symbolic character, many families resort to a cheaper solution: *For Divali, we had the same cloths as for Dasra* (R-18).

In terms of food safety, own processing and the procurement of staples from the villages are common actions. Another very simple strategy is avoidance, easily done with respect to outside food and as unhealthy classified instant foods. A pricier solution for the household lies in technology, for example in fridges, because *now we can go to the*

---

[21] In joint-families, the oldest brother and his wife have to take on most responsibility and hence also carry most of the burden. For example, they have to give the biggest share of their salary to the common good, while younger brothers can save for their childrens' education.

market which is further away, but cheaper than the nearby shop. Especially in summer, the curd which is kept in the fridge has a better taste. If it's too hot, we can't leave cooked vegetables outside, because they'll spoil till the night. Now, we keep them in the fridge and can have them at night or even the next day (R-29).

In general, the interview analysis has demonstrated that risks as well as strategies to mitigate stress are manifold. In box 2, an elder woman gives some of her evaluations on risk in the past and present. Box 3 gives an insight of risk handling in lower and higher economic classes. The remaining chapter tries to resume some observations of the analysis and to give some concluding remarks on the possibilities of a practical application as well as further study recommendations.

Box 2: Risk and worries of a 75 years old woman

When asked about risks and worries in her days and today, a Hindu woman, aged 75 and originally from Nizamabad, started narrating:

We used to grow food on fields and we only had to buy oil, salt and dal. Only rarely we sold corn, but we always sent food to the nearby relatives. When I was young and even after the marriage, I had hens, so we could have chicken whenever we liked. I fed them with left-over rice and grains. They were very tasty. There is a saying which means: 'When you have a hen at home it is like having dal all the time.' We never sold a hen or the eggs, it was all for self-consumption.

After the marriage, I stayed in a joint-family. They gave all the preference to men, so I worried about my children. For example, when the men had eaten all the curry, I felt bad for the children, but I wasn't allowed to slaughter another hen. I, as a mother was worried about the children, because all the preference was given to men. Whatever was left, went to the children and then to the women. Now it has changed. Preference is given to the children. I am happy with that.

Whenever we prepared food, we had to take good care. If the taste was not the same as usual, the husbands would throw it away together with the plates. So we women were always scared that they might not like what we cooked.

I didn't have to worry about the future, because all decisions were taken by the men. They even decided what we should cook. Women today have more worries, but keep them to themselves. I feel bad about today. Back then, everything was better, we didn't have any worries. These were the happy days. In those days, the seasons were in order, now the order has changed. The production has also changed. People have also changed, due to the changed production. People are becoming commercial and bad, so God punishes us. The public has to change (R-51).

Box 3: Risk and worries in lower and higher classes

Food security at one level (for example the male heads of households) does not necessarily imply food security of all household members. In fact, women usually eat whatever is left after their husbands and children had their share. Food security in lower income classes often is at risk and it is certainly a more pressing issue than food safety. For example, women go to central markets such as Bowanpalli, Hyderabad and collect the still usable remains from the soil, which is littered with smashed vegetables and cow dung.

And while the left-overs from festivals and functions are another important source of a cooked meal, a 22 years old girl of the upper class reported how girls are *on strict diets, some will only take liquids, some only fruits. I went on a diet myself. I should get married, but many say I'm too fat. Then I lost weight, felt sick and people said, I'm too thin!* (R-52)

Furthermore, while poor people increasingly face nourishment problems, even without taking quality in any consideration, the rich *don't have to worry about rising prices at all. We neither worry about food adulteration. We eat to die. We don't care about the health factor as long as it's tasty.* (ibid.) This attitude can also be observed when it comes to changing lifestyles and risks related to them: *Alcohol is definitely becoming a fashion and then a problem. People start drinking while socialising and end up being an alcoholic* (ibid.).

Thus, wealthy people have to deal with their own set of risks, usually relating to changing lifestyle fashions and therewith also new ideals, requirements and social pressures. On the other end of the economic ladder, poor people lead a daily struggle of survival. In between is the huge group of new middle classes, who all make a point in clearly distancing themselves from the poor: *Rising prices are a big problem for the poor families. They work daily for some Rs. 100 and have to spend all of that on rice!* (R-53)

6 Conclusion and further recommendations

A major problem of cities is their high degree of pollution, and other 'new risks' such as climate change often have severed consequences due to the urban structure of building and the like. These risks have in common that they are irreversible, difficult to observe and with global causality. Urban dwellers additionally are facing new socio-economic situations without the possibility of subsistency or traditionally proofed mitigation strategies. Development and modernisation in such a lively and heterogeneous megacity of tomorrow as Hyderabad hence means rapid and profound socio-cultural and economic alterations with the potential to mediate and shape perceived vulnerabilities, at the same time challenging the population's adaptive capacities and requiring an adjusted and flexible risk mitigation. In this frame, risk and vulnerability have to be seen as relational and social and the extent to which people are affected by vulnerability is designated by the "specific position of individuals and groups within the coordinates of society, space and time" (Bohle et al. 1993: 17, 18). This paraphrases the three dimensions of vulnerability: the risk of exposure, of inadequate capacities and of severe consequences (see Chapter 1). For example, in the monetary urban environment the costs of social events–paired with new desires–and education have gone up, while the support from the extended family is in decline (see Chambers 1989: 3; cited in: Bohle et al. 1993: 16). In general, losses in social capital as a form of social resilience (Adger 2000: 349) are common in a living situation where younger generations can no longer resort to their parents' and grandparents' wealth of experience and where neighbours often share neither origin nor past and where, instead, mistrust and socio-economic rivalry are the ruling factors. *I never ask neighbours, if I run out of something. I don't like them. I go to a kirana* (R-07). As the amount of experiences and knowledge affects the degree and manner of uncertainty, the urban setting with its array of new and fast changing realities and risks, paired with a diminution of social capital, represents a very specific ground for risk evaluations. One young woman who recently moved to the city explained: *In the village, they adjust and eat what they have. They do the field work, so whatever they have, they eat. Here, we have more things and different recipies and also more taste. But in the city, expenditures are also more. However, we get income for our work* (R-42).

And yet, risk research makes only sense where risks are perceived as such and the women's perception of risk was certainly not evident at first glance. Risks and threats seem to be interpreted as problematic situations, which naturally belong to the 'normal' difficulties in life where certain 'risky' decisions have to be taken due to lack of alternatives. Such situations, however, can often be contained through simple adjustments or correct–in the sense of culture conform–behaviour[22]. The principle of reciprocity, for example, is observed in various aspects, be it serving guests, sacrificing God or even the exchange of daughters, all strategies, which give reason to hope for an equitable or symbolic payback. What is more, the strongly perceived and lived hierarchical structure of the Indian society leads to the handover of responsibility to next higher instances, such as governmental institutions or the religious pantheon. This way, not only is there

---

[22] This „normalisation of risks" (Zwick & Renn 2002: 107) is not to be confounded with the findings of a study on risk perception in southern Germany, which allude to the fact that although Germans identify certain risks as such, they nevertheless consider them acceptable and unavoidable, therefore as *normal*.

no clear concept of risks, but the respondents also reject any responsibility for their own fate, a behaviour, quite contrary to the German dictum: 'Jeder ist seines Glückes Schmied' ('every man is the architect of his own future'). Nevertheless, it has to be kept in mind that this study can only detect trends and that it does not give overall valid statements. Therefore, further understanding of the ruling dynamics such as between the stoic resignation with its shift of responsibility towards others and yet at the same time a deep-rooted optimism, based on the believe in technology and own capabilities is needed, because all this leaves hardly room for a fully-fledged or even overcautious risk awareness. Moreover, access to good quality information is difficult and even experts lament that *institutions and departments are not interlinked, so we have no awareness-creation. No one knows what the other one does and how their works are interrelated. And we don't have enough access to institutional and governmental information which leads to many misconceptions, even among us scientists* (Interview with Radha Reddy, 23.11.2009)

This lack of risk awareness is even more surprising as the respondents belong to a double vulnerable group:

1. With an income range of Rs. 10,000 - 15,000, these households are still in a tenuous situation where they *have up and downs* (R-18). This becomes even more pronounced with new demands, which households can no longer satisfy when expenses for basic supplies are increasing. Thus, on the background of the subtle risk situation, also called the baseline vulnerability, these families are constantly exposed to latent or daily risks such as food adulteration and hygiene, price inflation, etc. Further threats are seasonal prices and budget fluctuations due to the monsoon or festival season. As these families usually do not dispose of large savings, their situation becomes severe when they are hit by contingent events ('shocks') such as serious health problems or the death of the husband as the earning person.

2. For present study, only women were questioned in a society, which is predominantly ruled by the male gender. In Indian lower middle class families, the woman is the caretaker of the house as well as of the physical and spiritual well-being of all household members. This means, for example, that men are often exempted from fasting and other religious duties, because they go out to earn money with which they sustain the family. Women, in contrast, sit at home and have the time and space to fulfil all religious duties (personal conversation with Radha Reddy, 23.11.2009). On the other hand, women consider themselves healthy as long as they are able to fulfil their social role (Kremer 2004: 84). When they need support in coping with stress, they seek it in various corners:

When dealing with problems, praying to God is very common. Or you have a good mutual understanding with your husbands. Nowadays, people also talk to friends or doctors. Most educated women want to come out of their problem somehow on themselves (R-31). This is a promising prospect in spite of some studies, which make a point in stating that women generally undervalue their own mitigation strategies as not good enough to make markable changes (Kremer 2004: 85). Most important, however, are the children, and any risks concerning them have an extremely high dread factor. Many tensions emerge from the interplay of the households' precarious financial situation, together with their tendency to adhere to traditional values and the ever multiplying demands of the consumeristic children. Yet, the society as a whole is undergoing ample changes, a fact which is recognised also by the parental generation: *The children's' uncle says that the society is changing, so we have to change as well. He's right, the society is changing, so why should we stop the children?* (F-47)

Yet, generally, these housewives talked about their worries of financial or hygienic character only on more specific enquiry. The persistent topic of chemicals, which are made responsible for the urban dwellers' poor health and the loss of taste were of specific importance. Or is this one way of turning abstract risks with often only latent consequences into something graspable? Yet also in Europe, every year, thousands of people die after the consumption of unhygienic edibles (due to bacteria and fungeses). However, although no one dies as a consequence of chemical preservatives, people still evaluate them as more hazardous (Renn et al. 2007: 86). Concerning the general alimentation, the nutritionist Radha Reddy notices that food-related problems are not as prevalent in lower income groups since they mainly follow a traditional diet. However, when families dilute curries and dal to save money, it certainly is threatening, because it means too little nutritional intake (interview, 23.11.2009).

An expedient suggestion is to enlarge the local food basket by indigenous millets and cereals, which are traditionally accepted and not only nutritious, yet also adapted to local climatic and ecological conditions. This way, ragi (finger millet) and jowar (sorghum) could help to ease the budget and emissions, while contributing at the same time to the consolidation of the people's health and cultural identity. Up to now, however, the national government does not show any interest in such a culturally and ecologically sound option, because it wants to further promote its heavily subsidised wheat from the North of the country and so far, it has been successful, as many families turn to the preparation of wheat chapatti when they are short of money. A further option could be seen in the enhancement of urban agriculture, which would contribute to the inhabitants' food security as well as the local urban climate. However, to achieve any positive effects, its stigmatisation of being unhealthy and polluted has to be overcome.

To recapitulate, risks and crisis open up chances for long-term betterments and improvements. Yet, such improvements have to be embedded in deeper lying socio-cultural structures and can only enhance local resilience when decision makers include the lower class population in their planning (also see Bohle 2008: 436-437). It is hereby important to understand which countermeasures are socially and culturally accepted and to recognise the important role women play as multiplicators and transmitters of knowledge and behaviour through their educational legacy. Yet, when risk is understood as a social construct, its evaluation is performed through ascription processes and can never be seen independent of the perceiver's social world. Thus, a holistic approach to resilience needs a more detailed and comprehensive study of risks and vulnerabilities throughout the course of a whole year, which, for example, would include potential seasonal irregularities, such as the yearly inflation in food prices due to the monsoon rains. Furthermore, as the Indian conception of 'future' turned out to be different from our western idea, it is advisable to keep this crisis oriented perspective with all its implications for the people's opinion on their own capacities to change the future in mind and, accordingly to also have a closer look at the religious dimensions of 'fate' and 'destiny'.

The risks and their consequences treated in this study are latent processes and thus, albeit their everyday presence, difficult to assess. This shows in the small number of such studies, although it resembles a wide field for future environmental health research, especially in conjunction with climate change. Here, the use of transdisciplinary methods could help to aptly assess political and economic structures as well as emic perceptions. This way, present analysis is an attempt to contribute to current scientific discussion on risks and their evaluation from an inductive perspective.

References

Adger, W.N. 2000. "Social and ecological resilience: are they related?" *Progress in Human Geography* 24(3): 347–364.

Akbar, S. 2009. "Bt threat to native brinjal." Deccan Chronicle, 05.11.2009.

Bayerische Rück (ed.). 1993. *Risiko ist ein Konstrukt. Wahrnehmungen zur Risikowahrnehmung.* Reihe: Gesellschaft und Unsicherheit; Band 2. Knesebeck, München.

Beck, U. 2007. *Risikogesellschaft – auf dem Weg in eine andere Moderne.* Suhrkamp, Frankfurt.

Blaikie, P. 1994. *At risk: natural hazards, people's vulnerability, and disasters.* Routledge, London.

Blaikie, P. and H. Brookfield. 1987. *Land Degradation and Society.* Development Studies; University Paperbacks, Methuen, London.

Bohle, H.-G. 2008. "Leben mit Risiko – Resilience als neues Paradigma für die Risikowelten von morgen." In *Naturrisiken und Sozialkatastrophen.* edited by Felgentreff, C. and T. Glade: 435–442. Spektrum Akademischer Verlag, Berlin, Heidelberg.

Bohle, H.-G. and T. Glade. 2008: "Vulnerabilitätskonzepte in Sozial- und Naturwissenschaften." In *Naturrisiken und Sozialkatastrophen.* edited by Felgentreff, C. and T. Glade: 99–120. Spektrum Akademischer Verlag, Berlin, Heidelberg.

Bohle, H.-G., T.E. Downing, J.O. Field and F.N. Ibrahim. 1993. "Coping with Vulnerability and Critically – Case Studies on Food-Insecure People and Places." In *Freiburger Studien zur Geographischen Entwicklungsforschung.* edited by H.-G. Bohle. Verlag breitenbach, Saarbrücken.

Chambers, R. 1989. "Editorial Introduction: Vulnerability, Coping and Policy." *IDS Bulletin* 20(2):1–7.

Chapman, G. et al. 1997. *Environmentalism and the mass media: the North-South divide.* London.

Chengappa, S. 2009. "Value fashion retailing becomes fashionable." Deccan Chronicle, 02.11.2009.

Deccan Chronicle (DC). 2009. Staff Reporter:

15.10.2009a: Centre refuses rice for YSR's scheme – Delhi gives wheat, AP says it won't serve purpose.

15.10.2009b: Grow super fine rice: CM.

20.10.2009: Traders mix ghee with animal fat.

22.10.2009a: The vegetable war. The DC debate: Bt brinjal is a good idea, it will help enhance food production.

22.10.2009b: Recession spreading epidemic!

23.10.2009a: Inflation up on costly food.

23.10.2009b: Dengue cases on the rise.

29.10.2009: Food crisis stares at state.

01.11.2009: Spurious ghee is a health hazard.

02.11.2009a: Unhygienic food joints: pose health problems.

02.11.2009b: Excessive soda bad for kidney.

09.11.2009: Food prices will fall by March, says Montek.

10.11.2009a: Farmers end live.

10.11.2009b: Hooked on to party pills – Youngsters are opting for quick fixes to lose weight before big dos.

15.11.2009, Magazine: Best spots for bandi Chinese.

16.11.2009: What should be done to prevent the spread of viral fevers?

21.11.2009: No import of rice for now, says Centre.

24.11.2009: Soaring prices take eggs off common man's menu.

25.11.2009: Diabetes causes obesity.

27.11.2009, Magazine: Saturday is for starving – Youngsters prefer starving themselves on weekends in a bid to look svelte at parties and squeeze into their LBDs.

28.11.2009: City wears a festive look for Id.

Dittrich, C. and F. Krueger (eds.). 2000. "Urbanization, Vulnerability and Resource Management in Developing Countries." *APT-Report*, No. 11, January 2000. Freiburg i.Br.

Dombrowsky, W.R. 2008. "Zur Entstehung der soziologischen Katastrophenforschung – eine wissenshistorische und –soziologische Reflexion." In *Naturrisiken und Sozialkatastrophen.* edited by C. Felgentreff and T. Glade: 63–76. Spektrum Akademischer Verlag, Berlin, Heidelberg.

Douglas, M. 1994. *Risk and blame: essays in cultural theory.* Routledge, London.

Douglas, M. and A. Wildavsky. 1983. *Risk and culture: an essay on the selection of technological and environmental dangers.* Univ. of California Press, Berkeley, CA.

Elverfeldt, K.v., T. Glade and R. Dikau. 2008. "Naturwissenschaftliche Gefahren- und Risikoanalyse." In *Naturrisiken und Sozialkatastrophen.* edited by C. Felgentreff and T. Glade: 31–46. Spektrum Akademischer Verlag, Berlin, Heidelberg.

Felgentreff, C. and T. Glade (eds.). 2008. *Naturrisiken und Sozialkatastrophen.* Spektrum Akademischer Verlag, Berlin, Heidelberg.

Felgentreff, C. and W. R. Dombrowsky. 2008. "Hazard-, Risiko- und Katastrophenforschung." In *Naturrisiken und Sozialkatastrophen.* edited by C. Felgentreff and T. Glade: 13–30. Spektrum Akademischer Verlag, Berlin, Heidelberg.

Griffiths, J., M. Rao, F. Adshead and A. Thorpe (eds.). 2009. *The Health Practitioner's Guide to Climate Change – Diagnosis and Cure.* Earthscan, London, Sterling.

Hofmann, R. and C. Dittrich. 2009. "Changing Food Culture in Globalising Hyderabad." Available at: www.sustainable-hyderabad.in.

Human Development Report (HDR). 2007/2008. *Fighting Climate Change: Human Solidarity in a Divided World.* UNDP; Palgrave Macmillan, New York.

Hyderabad Times. 17.11.2009. The importance of vitamin E.

India Meteorological Department (IMD). 2009. "Southwest Monsoon 2009 End-of-Season Report (Updated)." www.imd.gov.in/section/nhac/dynamic/endseason report09.pdf [23-02-10].

IPC Food Sovereignty. 2010. www.foodsovereingty.org [28-01-2010].

Jacob, K. S. 2009. "Alcohol politics, policies and public health." The Hindu, 03.11.2009.

Jungermann, H. and P. Slovic. 1993. "Charakteristika individueller Risikowahrnehmung." In *Risiko ist ein Konstrukt – Wahrnehmungen zu Risikowahrnehmung.* edited by Bayerische Rück: 93–107. Reihe: Gesellschaft und Unsicherheit, Bd. 2; Knesebeck, München.

Kasperson R. et al. 1988. "The Social Amplification of Risk – A Conceptual Framework." *Risk Analysis* 8(2): 177–187.

Kremer, A. 2004. "Urbane Umwelt und Gesundheit: Exposition und Risikowahrnehmung vulnerabler Bevölkerungsgruppen in Pondicherry, Indien." ULB Bonn; http://hss.ulb.uni-bonn.de/diss_online/abc/k.htm [07-09-2009].

Krüger, F. 1997. "Urbanisierung und Verwundbarkeit in Botswana." *Sozioökonomische Prozesse in Asien und Afrika* 1, Pfaffenweiler.

Lange, H. and L. Meier (eds.). 2009. *Globalizing Lifestyles, Consumerism, and Environmental Concern – The Case of the New Middle Classes.* Springer publications.

Leppin, A. 1994. *Bedingungen des Gesundheitsverhaltens. Risikowahrnehmung und persönliche Ressourcen.* Juventa Verlag, Weinheim und München.

Manyena, S. B. 2006. "The concept of resilience revisited." *Disasters* 30(4): 433–450.

Milbert, I. 2009. "Policy Dimensions of Human Security and Vulnerability Challenges. The Case of Urban India." In *Facing global environmental change - environmental, human, energy, food, health and water security concepts.* edited by H.-G. Brauch: 233–242. Berghof Foundation. Springer, Berlin; Heidelberg.

Mukherjee, S. 2009. "City slips on adulterated edible oils." Deccan Chronicle, 01.11.2009.

Noe, C. 2007. "Health Vulnerability städtischer Marginalgruppen in Colombia, Sri Lanka." *Studien zur Geographischen Entwicklungsforschung* 34; Saarbrücken.

Nuttall, M. 2009. "Living in a World of Movement: Human Resilience to Environmental Instability in Greenland." In *Anthropology and Climate Change – From Encounters to Actions.* edited by S. Crate and M. Nuttall: 292–310. Left Coast Press, Walnut Creek, CA.

Oppili, P. and R. Kannan. 2009. "Custon officials concerned over import of adulterated food products." The Hindu, 19.10.2009.

Osho Foundation. 2009. "There's no other way to live, but dangerously." Deccan Chronicle Magazine, 15.11.2009.

Pandeya, R. C. 1992. "Indian Attitude towards Nature." *GeoJournal* 26(2): 135–138.

Pheroze, L. V. 2009. "Coimbatore ryots give up paddy for cocoa." The Hindu, 26.11.2009.

Pidgeon et al. 1992. "Risk Perception." In *Royal Society Study Group: Risk: Analysis, Perception and Management.* The Royal Society, London.

Popkin, B. M. 1999. *Urbanization, Lifestyle Changes and the Nutrition Transition.* 2020 Focus No. 03 – Brief 07, IFPRI. http://www.ifpri.org/2020/focus/focus03/focus03_07.asp [28-02-2010].

Prabu, M.J. 2009. "Mobile helps find right price for farmers produce." The Hindu, 05.11.2009.

Putnam, R. (ed.). 2002. *Democracies in flux: the evolution of social capital in comtemporary society.* Oxford University Press, Oxford, New York.

Rajendra, Ranjani. 2009. "Young India turns obese. Doctors reveal that the city's youth is hit by the 'software syndrome'." Deccan Chronicle, 16.10.2009.

Rajiv, Dr. 2009. "It's not all about junk – Contrary to common belief, some food from the West are healthier than what cooks in Indian kitchen." The Hindu Metro Plus, 31.10.2009.

Reddy, Gayatri. 2009. "Ageorexia plagues society – Many people want to look young forever and the thought of looking old gives them nightmares." Deccan Chronicle Magazine, 27.11.2009.

Reddy, Sudhakar U. 2009.

a: "39 suicides a day in AP." Deccan Chronicle, 18.11.2009.

b: "AP, victim of climate change." Deccan Chronicle, 23.10.2009.

Renn, O., P.-J. Schweizer, P.-J., M. Dreyer and A. Klinke. 2007. *Risiko – Über den gesellschaftlichen Umgang mit Unsicherheiten.* oekom Verlag, München.

Renn, O. and B. Rohrmann (eds.). 2000. *Technology, Risk, and Society, Vol. 13: Cross-Cultural Risk Perception. A Survey of Empirical Studies.* Dordrecht.

Royal Society Study Group. 1992. *Risk: Analysis, Perception and Management.* The Royal Society, London.

Sahai, S. 2009. "Bt brinjal can awaken a sleeping poison." Deccan Chronicle, 05.11.2009.

Slovic, P. 2000. "The perception of risk." *Science, New Series* 236(4799) (Apr. 17, 1987): 280–285.

Slovic, P., S. Lichtenstein and B. Fischhoff. 1984. "Modeling the societal impact of fatal accidents." *Management Science* 30: 464–474.

Swaminathan, M. S. 2009. "The media and the farm sector." The Hindu, 11.11.2009.

The Hindu. 2009. Staff Reporter:

15.10.2009: Mobile rythu bazars to sell onion.

22.10.2009: This year's rice crops hit by climate change.

03.11.2009: Holistic approach needed to ensure food security.

07.11.2009: Food inflation rises to 14.55 per cent.

09.11.2009, Metro Plus: Focus is on fitness – Sports, medicine specialist David V. Rajan on medical care and fitness training.

13.11.2009a: Of raising prices and diluted menus.

13.11.2009b: Naidu focuses on price rise.

14.11.2009: Prevalence of diabetes higher in South India.

16.11.2009: Depression common among obese children.

17.11.2009: Consumers not getting their fair price: Mukherjee.

17.11.2009, Metro Plus: Catching food trends – Chefs and journalists thrash out the debate about Indian culinary trends.

20.11.2009: Wine shops, bars to remain closed.

22.11.2009, Magazine: Red Power.

21.11.2009: Expert blames corporate sector for increasing obesity.

23.11.2009a: Move to boost rice cultivation.

23.11.2009b: 200 contestants linked to liquor trade.

25.11.2009a: Five distilleries get nod to enhance production.

25.11.2009b: Mass prayer on November 28.

The Times of India (TNN). 29.01.2010: RBI signals CRR hike as food prices rise again. http://timesofindia.indiatimes.com/biz/india-business/RBI-signals-CRR-hike-as-food-prices-rise-again/articleshow/5511294.cms [23-02-10].

Varley, A. (ed.). 1994. *Disasters, development and environment*. J. Wiley, Chichester.

Vydhianathan, S. 2009. "Food subsidy set to cross Rs. 4,000 crore." The Hindu, 27.11.2009.

Watts, M. and H.-G. Bohle. 1993a. "The Space of Vulnerability: the Causal Structure of Hunger and Famine." *Progress in Human Geography* 17(1): 43–67.

Watts, M. and H.-G. Bohle. 1993b. "Hunger, Famine and the Space of Vulnerability." *GeoJournal* 30(2): 117–125.

Wisner, B. and H.R. Luce. 1993. "Disaster Vulnerability – Geographical Scale and Existential Reality." In *Worlds of pain and hunger: geographical perspectives on disaster vulnerability and food security.* edited by H.-G. Bohle: 13–54. Third international famine workshop at Tufts University, from 4 to 7 Aug., 1992. Saarbrücken; Fort Lauderdale: Breitenbach. Freiburger Studien zur Geographischen Entwicklungsländerforschung, No. 5.

Wisner, B., P. Blaikie, T. Cannon and I. Davis. 2008. *At risk: natural hazards, people's vulnerability and disasters*. 2. ed., repr. Routledge, London, New York.

Wildavsky, A. 1993. "Vergleichende Untersuchung zur Risikowahrnehmung: Ein Anfang." In *Risiko ist ein Konstrukt – Wahrnehmungen zu Risikowahrnehmung.* edited by Bayerische Rück. Reihe: Gesellschaft und Unsicherheit, Bd. 2; Knesebeck, München.

World Health Organization. 2002. "The World Health Report 2002 – Reducing Risks, Promoting Healthy Life." www.who.int [12-02-10].

Zwick, M. and O. Renn. 2002. *Perception and evaluation of risks – Findings of the 'Baden-Württemberg Risk Survey 2001*. Joint Working Report by the Center of Technology Assessment in Baden-Württemberg and the University of Stuttgart, Sociology of Technologies and Environment, No. 203.